Copyright © 2021 by Sverre Steensen

All rights reserved. This book or any portion thereof may not be reproduced or used in any manner whatsoever without the express written permission of the publisher except for the use of brief quotations in a book review.

First Printing, 2021

ISBN: 9798501479654
Imprint: Independently Published
Author: Sverre Steensen

Upstart Garage Media
Landgangen 2
0252 Oslo, Norway

www.upstartgarage.com

Check out our other book titles
on www.upstartgarage.com

Table of Contents

Introduction 3
1 - Make the ultimate advent calendar 4
2 - What is the best business idea - become a YouTuber or blogger? 9
3 - Discuss the restaurant business while waiting for your meal 10
4 - Study ads to learn communication 12
5 - Is starting a used toy market a great idea? 14
6 - Psychological prices: Is $19.95 cheaper than $20.05? 15
7 - How to create amazing inventions? 16
8 - Can you write better e-mails? 17
9 - Ice cream for a business plan 18
10 - Should you fire your best friend? 20
11 - Solving your grandparent's problems? 21
12 - What is a good logo? 22
13 - What is the best business idea - homework tutor or gaming teacher? 24
14 - Watch Jerry Maguire with your kid 25
15 - Is creating a meal kit for kids to cook a good idea? 26
16 - Play the game Rollercoaster Tycoon 27
17 - To-do lists for kids 28
18 - Understanding cost and margin 29
19 - Develop crazy ideas 31
20 - What is your movie popcorn? 32
21 - Build the theme park of your dreams 33
22 - Invest with your kids 37
23 - Business Sunday: Launch a waffle and lemonade stand before lunch 39
24 - What is the best idea - a slime factory or a bath bomb factory? 42
25 - What is cross-selling? 43

26 - Watch infomercials together	44
27 - Is starting a temp agency for kids a good idea?	46
28 - Brainstorming with your kids	47
29 - Raising 1,000 dollars to start a new venture	49
30 - Understanding price elasticity	50
31 - Solving your parent's problems	52
32 - What questions to ask when hiring?	53
33 - Understanding scale advantages	54
34 - The elevator pitch	56
35 - Let your kid be your manager	57
36 - Can you improve the TV ad?	59
37 - Is creating a homemade strawberry and raspberry jam a great idea?	60
38 - How do Netflix and Spotify make money?	61
39 - What is his/her occupation?	63
40 - The idea journal	64
41 - What is a good brand name?	65
42 - Should you invest in a company with a cool product?	66
43 - Who in your class would you hire for help?	68
44 - Watch Dragon's Den and Shark Tank together	69
45 - Start a business on a car trip	71
46 - Create your first budget	74
47 - How to handle all the cash	76
48 - Create a new logo for Coca-Cola, Nike, and McDonald's	77
49 - Understanding USPs	78
50: What is the best idea—become the neighborhood baker or candy maker?	79
51 - Teach your kid to set goals and achieve them	80
52 - Find problems we want solved and give us a price	81
53 - Is creating a homework station a good idea?	82
54 - Learn to do a SWOT analysis	83
55 - The Not To-do list for kids	85
56 - Play the game Rise of Industry	86
57 - Build a candy factory	87
58 - How to read a balance sheet?	89
59 - How to measure a business?	91
60 - What is the best idea - grass cutting or fruit/berry picking?	93
61 - How to serve a shit sandwich?	94
62 - How does a bank work?	95
63 - Is selling spaghetti-filled pancakes at school a great idea?	96
64 - Your school has to buy a product from you. What do they buy?	97
65 - How many razor blades are sold?	98
66 - Is a company that's losing money worth zero?	99
67 - Why offer a money-back guarantee?	100
68 - How to solve your friend's problems?	101

69 - What is upselling? 102
70 - Watch The Pursuit of Happiness together 103
71 - Play Monopoly together 104
72 - Watch Moneyball together 106
73 - What is the best idea - become a magician or balloon maker? 107
74 - Is personalized books for kids a good idea? 108
75 - How much does TV advertisement cost? 109
76 - How does a YouTuber make money? 110
77 - What is the market for house cleaning services? 111
78 - What is the purpose of a business? 112
79 - How will companies fare if a catastrophe occurs in the world? 113
80 - What is the best idea - dog walking or plant watering business? 114
81 - How to value a company? 115
82 - Watch Big starring Tom Hanks together 116
83 - Is buying used Legos and reselling them a great idea? 117
84 - Is developing and selling the ultimate super soaker a great idea? 118
85 - What is the best business idea - car washer or bicycle fixer? 119
86 - Is a gift advice business a great idea? 120
87- Arrange a business playdate for your kid and their friends 121
88 - What is the best business idea - helping seniors or cleaning houses? 123
89 - How to structure a retail store 124
90 - The five whys of business... 126
91 - Create a subscription business 127
92 - How to make the investor pitch? 128
93 - How to evaluate ideas? 129
94 - Should you create an app for household duties? 131
95 - Create a marketing campaign for school 133
96 - Is a parenting guide a good idea? 135
97 - A/B testing with your kids 136
98 - Become a master negotiator... 138
99- What is the best business idea - a tech wiz or website developer? 140

Introduction

If you can inspire your kids today and change their life trajectory for the better, will you do it? If you say "yes," then this book is for you.

Kids learn many valuable skills at school, online, from their parents and grandparents, but few are taught business principles before they are in their twenties, except for some of the world's most successful entrepreneurs. These millionaires were exposed to business fundamentals at a young age, either by their own initiative or from resources around them.

This book's objective is not to train a young generation of entrepreneurs but to inspire you and your kid to reflect on business practices and society together. By exploring these chapters, you will have fun and learn together as a family.

The book can be read by you, the parent, from cover to cover to pick out your favorite exercises and topics to later discuss with your kid. Alternatively, you and your young ones could read the book together, or simply flip through it to pick the most exciting sections and try the exercises.

All of the examples and activities in this book have been tested and proven to teach valuable business lessons and inspire kids from the age of 6 to 16—sometimes much older. So, get ready to inspire your kids and possibly change their life or career trajectory. Maybe your kid will thank you in their first interview after taking their company public.

1 - Make the ultimate advent calendar

Kids love an advent calendar. You now have the opportunity to give your children a unique calendar to inspire a great learning experience.

Curious?

The ultimate advent calendar aims to pique your kid's interest in companies, investment, and society, not to turn them into Gordon Gekko miniatures from the film Wall Street. You should create a calendar for them filled with stocks and possibly other investments. Beginning December 1, each day the advent calendar holds a new stock that may spark a good conversation. On December 24, the kids get all the stocks and can sell them, or they can hold them for another month, possibly years, before they cash in. You can make the calendar multiple ways. Here's how to create it:

- Buy the stocks in your name with your stock account. The advantage of this approach is that you actually buy the stock. The disadvantage is that you have to pay trading fees.

- An easier option is to "buy" the stock by writing the date in one column of a spreadsheet, the name of the stock in the next, then the price, and finally, a link to the page showing the price of that particular stock. It will look like a real stock purchase to your kid, and you don't have the transaction costs.

As long as you give your kid the correct amount of money when he/she wants to sell, this method appears "real" to your kid.

- Finally, you can write down all the stocks and their prices on a paper calendar. Draw 24 squares on a large piece of paper with their number and content hidden. When you remove the hider you placed on top of each square (possibly a Post-it Note®), the square lists the company name, and then your kid writes down in the square the share price of that particular company from the previous day.

On December 24, your kid has received 24 shares. He/she can now decide what to do with them. Sell or keep them in the hope that they will increase in value. Every Sunday, you can check to see if the stocks have gained or lost value and discuss whether to keep or sell them. When your kid wants to sell, look up the new prices and hand your kid the money from the stock sale.

Make sure the stocks you buy are not too expensive. That will drive up the value of the calendar. Remember, you can mix it up with penny stocks, which may still be exciting companies. As December progress, there is a chance that your kid may want you to invest in a specific stock. It may be stocks in computer games companies, or perhaps toy or clothing brands. Try to include some of these companies in the calendar.

You can also give the kid a daily budget, for example, $10, and let them "shop" a stock for certain dates. If you are not actually buying the stock but maintaining the stock's value in a paper calendar or a spreadsheet, then you can give your kid 10% of a stock. It can be more fun to own 10% of the Apple stock than 100% of one stock in a company they don't know.

When it comes to selecting stocks, you have many options to consider:

- Buy stocks in companies and brands your kids know. It's a good starting point for interesting discussions.
- Find stocks that are controversial to stimulate good learning opportunities.
- Select some stocks that have huge risks in order to discuss the possibility of bankruptcy.

With the basics down, you are ready for the important stuff. The discussions and reflections you have with your children after they have opened the calendar. Here are some ideas:

- *Who sets the price of a stock?* The cost of a stock is set when buyers and sellers meet and agree on a price. Investors selling shares of a stock believe the price of the stock will drop. The ones buying the stock expect it to rise in price.
- *Should we invest in stocks that do good, or just focus on good investments?* This question can lead to a good discussion on the purpose of investing and why companies exist in the first place. Is the role of a company just to stay within the law and make money for its shareholders?
- *Is a stock with a low price cheaper than a stock with a high price?* No, the share price has nothing to do with company value (this might be difficult for kids to understand). You have to also consider the number of shares in the company.
- *Can the price of a stock be negative?* No, a stock can only reach zero. Then the company is considered bankrupt.

- *Is a company with a popular product a better investment than one with a boring product?* Not necessarily. The popularity of the product has often driven the price up, making it a less attractive investment.
- *What do you think drives the price up or down for the company?* Many factors impact the performance of a stock. You have macro factors (elections, wars, trade wars, political changes, etc.); industry factors (new regulations, other companies' performance, etc.); and finally, company-specific issues (sales, results, management, etc.).
- *Is it better to buy the product or the stock?* This is an interesting discussion. Does your kid want the product that gets old, or would they rather own a small part of all future products?
- *What do you believe will happen to this company going forward?* Whether a stock moves up or down depends not on what has happened but rather on future results. What do you believe will happen to the company from now on?
- *What makes a good company, and what makes a great company?* You just bought a small piece of a company; is it a good or a truly great company?

If you want to add other elements to the calendar than just stocks, here are some ideas and their rationale:

- *Currency* – You can add a dollar, a euro, or a Norwegian krone. Money, like stock, varies in value and is a good starting point for discussions on why you believe it's a good idea to keep the euro or sell it. If you are uncertain of the macro effects that impact currency, look it up online with your kids—read and discuss.

- *Barrel of oil* – Oil is one of the most important commodities in the world. Its prices fluctuate based on demand and the stability or instability of the world economy. It can be a great starting point for interesting discussions.
- *A gram of gold* – Gold has a long history of being valuable. Why is that, and why do some investors think it is smart to own if companies fall in value? You can find many perspectives on owning gold on YouTube. Letting your kid own a small piece of gold that they can sell when they want can inspire their thinking about business, society, money, and value.
- *A bushel of wheat* – Put a bushel of wheat and its price into a day in the calendar. How is it possible to own wheat without owning a farm? Get ready for a transformational talk with your kid.
- *Sugar* – Your kid probably loves sugar! So, let them own it, and not only consume it. Check how you can invest in sugar and discuss why the price may go up or down.
- *Bitcoins* – Buy 0,1% of a bitcoin to the calendar. What on earth is bitcoin, and why does it have value?
- *Coffee futures* – You can put coffee in the calendar and discuss what drives the prices up and down.

Try to develop a daily routine for the ultimate advent calendar. A suggestion may be to open that day's calendar element in the morning. You can then have an exciting discussion when you put the kids to bed. When they see your engagement in their life, it will be an experience they will cherish for the rest of their life.

Consider posting your experience on social media. It's a truly unique calendar that may inspire other parents to make something similar.

2 - What is the best business idea - become a YouTuber or blogger?

Ask your kid what business they would like to start, a YouTube channel or becoming a blogger.

Establishing a YouTube channel can be a profitable business for both young and old. If you have something to say and people subscribe and watch your content, it's possible to make a good living from ads and various sponsors of your channel.

A blogger writes about specific subjects, like cooking or sports, or their life in general. If the blog becomes popular, you make money from ads and different types of sponsors posted on the blog.

Here are a few questions to probe the reasoning of your kid's decision:

- Which business do you think will be the most fun to start?
- Where would you make the most money?
- What is the easiest to start?
- Do these businesses have the same customers or are they different?

Is your kid inspired to start one of these business the next weekend?

3 - Discuss the restaurant business while waiting for your meal

Waiting for food at a restaurant is the perfect time and place to teach your kids about business. Here's some inspiration:

- How would you change the menu? Which dishes would you add and which would you remove? What do you think of the prices? Do you think the prices are too high, too low, or just right? What do you think would happen to the restaurant if you doubled the prices or reduced the costs in half? A restaurant is not selling food to anyone passing by. Which customer group is this restaurant target?

- What do you think of the employees working in the restaurant? Would you have hired the people working at this restaurant? Why? Do you believe they are doing a good job? Do they have uniforms? If so, do you like the look of the uniforms? Would you train the employees differently?

- Now estimate seatings per day. Do they have one seating for lunch and two or three seating times for dinner? Then consider the occupancy rate. Is the restaurant half full or full? If the restaurant has three seating times and 20 tables that are only half full, then the number of tables served per day is about 30.

- Now consider the average price a table is paying. Discuss and see what number you end up with. Finally, multiply the number of tables with the average price per table, and you have the daily revenues.

- Do you think this restaurant is making money? To estimate if the restaurant is making money, you need to understand its cost. To calculate the cost, you first need to know its structure. Have a discussion on the cost of food and drinks. In most restaurants, it's between 25-35%. Use 30% to make the calculation easier. The personal or labor cost is typically around 30%. You can calculate it in more detail by counting how many people work in the restaurant, multiplied by how much money they make. Then, consider the rent. It's typically somewhere between 5-10% of revenues. Think about marketing. Have you seen ads for this restaurant? How much do you guess they are spending on marketing in a year? Finally, there are the miscellaneous cost that can be a few percentages of the cost and includes (accounting, electricity, tech systems, etc.).

What type of restaurant would you create if you had all the freedom in the world? Challenge your kid on what type of restaurant they would like to start. You can inspire them with some thought-provoking questions:

- What food do you think is most popular?

- If you were the cook in a restaurant, what foods would you serve?

- What if you were to create a restaurant for kids? How would it be different from regular restaurants? How would you decorate the restaurant?

4 - Study ads to learn communication

Whenever you have time, it's fun to look at advertisements together. It can be ads in newspapers, magazines, or online. The purpose is to teach and reflect on how ads communicate, sell, and convince an audience. Being knowledgeable about these effects will make your kid more aware of how they are being influenced by companies every day.

Here are some of the questions and issues you can discuss when studying advertisements together:

- Who is this advertisement made for? Who is the target customer? Few ads are created to appeal to everyone. Most have a single type of customer in mind. Can you guess who the company is thinking of and trying to reach?

- What is the main message that the ad is trying to get across? Examine how they use headlines, text, images, and sales offers to convince the reader to buy their product.

- An ad can trigger different emotions, humor, facts, curiosity, and so on. What emotions is this ad trying to tap into?

- If it's an ad for a product, what are the unique selling points (USPs)? For a smartphone, it could be the screen size, camera functions, speed, etc.

- Ads use many tricks to convince the audience. How are they telling you that it's a good offer? A common practice is to show before and after prices, limited-time discounts, number of sales, etc. A successful ad creates a sense of urgency and a call to action from the viewer. What techniques are used? "Offer valid until…" or "Valid as long as stock lasts."

- Is the ad building a brand, selling hard, or a mix of both? Many ads in glossy magazines are more about brand building. They use little text, large, beautifully staged images, and no prices. Others are more direct, with text like "buy now," listing prices, and so on.

How could you make the ad you see better?

- Changing the headline.
- Changing the image.
- Changing the text.
- Changing the offer.
- Changing the whole concept.

5 - Is starting a used toy market a great idea?

Ask your kid if they think it's a good idea to start a venture that collects used toys in the neighborhood and sells them to other kids for a low price?

The money from sales is split between you (the seller) and the previous toy owner. After explaining the concept, discuss:

- What is the largest challenge with this business?
- How many toys would it be possible to sell in a month? How much money might you make?
- If you were to start this venture, do you think it would be successful?

6 - Psychological prices: Is $19.95 cheaper than $20.05?

Walk into a store with your kid and look at the prices of products. Why are they priced the way they are? Look at similar products and discuss which ones the store wants you to buy, based upon price and location in the store.

As you walk around stores, you will see prices ending in .99 and .95. Is there a difference between $19.95 and $20.05? Of course, there is, but the difference is more than just ten cents.

Welcome to the world of psychological pricing. There are many ways to price a product. It may be set based upon company cost, competitors' prices, or what price the company believes customers are willing to pay. When a company is close to the price range, they want to sell a product for, it's time to consider psychological factors. The most obvious price points are: $9.99, $99.99, or $999.

Staying one tick below a round number is a tactic used in all markets. It tricks the customer's mind into believing the price is significantly lower than what it really is. There are also local variants that depend on the type of bills used in that particular market. For instance, there are $20 bills in the US, which leads to popular price points of $19.95, $39.95, $59.95. In other markets, there are 100 and 500 denomination bills, making those important price points.

7 - **How to create amazing inventions?**

Kids love to come up with ideas for new inventions. Have your kids come up with ideas for innovations that can be sold to customers. Instead of giving them free rein, impose limitations. A narrower focus is good for harnessing creativity. For instance, give them one of the tasks below to complete in thirty minutes while you make dinner. Then, they can present their invention with words and drawings during dinner.

- Do you have an idea for an invention that will help me prepare dinner?
- Develop an invention to make school lunches taste better or be more fun?
- Do you have ideas for inventions that will make parents believe their kid is sleeping when they are actually awake?
- You are continually outgrowing your clothes. Can you solve this problem?
- Do you have ideas for inventions to help reduce the use of plastic?
- Can you make the world's best alarm clock to wake you up in the morning?
- Young kids hate to wash their hair. Can you solve the problem with a new invention?

- Can you make the world's coolest face mask for kids?
- Develop an invention to make homework easier to complete?
- Can you create the best Christmas gift for next year?
- Can you make the number-one favorite gift for kids your age?

8 - Can you write better e-mails?

You receive lots of e-mails trying to sell you products or services. Read them together, and look at the text, images, and product offers. It's a fun exercise in communication, selling, and understanding of how advertising works.

- What is the tone of the e-mail? Are they trying to make it personal, fun, serious, and so on?
- Do you like the title? Does it make you curious to click to open the message and read further?
- What is the purpose of the e-mail, and what is it aiming for you to do?

If your kid likes the exercise, they can try to write a sales e-mail themselves, or try changing one you have received from another company.

9 - Ice cream for a business plan

Kids love ice cream. Use their desire for the cold delight to inspire them in a creative endeavor. The concept is easy—*give your kid a scoop of ice cream for creating a business plan.*

For the reward to be within your kid's grasp, the exercise should not take more than thirty minutes to complete. It's fun, engaging, and the kid gets a good learning experience. It will teach them to be creative, structured, thoughtful, improve their writing, and the ability to present—all valuable business and life skills. Before you start, you need to explain what a business plan is.

- A business plan describes the business idea and how to implement it. It may be original, a new idea or starting something similar to other companies. It can be a new product, a new theme park, a local restaurant, or selling a product or service that already exists. You can mention some examples to inspire them or ask them to develop solutions to problems they have or see others have. Tell them to write a paragraph to describe their idea and why they think it will be valuable to customers. The text may be supplemented with drawings. This is the absolute minimum they have to do to deserve ice cream.

- Have them describe what they intend to charge for their product or service, etc. The benefit of them setting the price is that they have to consider how much value their offering creates and what customers could be willing to pay for their offer.
- Finally, they should briefly describe how they would go about setting up such a business.
- When they have completed their business plan, have them present it to you aloud. Presenting will help your kid improve their ability to distill the essence of a message and communicate it out loud to others.

Now, give them the ice cream without asking too many questions and giving too much feedback. If you do this exercise many times, you can challenge your kid more. If they want to spend more time on their business plan, they can include these elements in their plan:

- Who are their customers (it should not be everyone; it should be more specific)?
- What is their market (the geographical area and the customers within that area)?
- How would they market their business (in what channels and what is the message)?
- Make a budget for the business (what do they expect in revenues per month, and what are the different costs associated with it?)
- What would their store, posters, T-shirts, etc. look like (they can add drawings of their business if they want)?

Make sure to give praise. Don't comment on misspellings or things you find to be "crazy" or impossible in the business plan. After you do the exercise multiple times, your kid will gain confidence and be more daring in their creativity.

The last point is that creativity often flows better if there are limitations or boundaries instead of free reign. Creating a business plan for a new restaurant, or selling something new to kids at school, is often easier for kids to understand and make a business plan for than telling them to create any type of business in the world. The limits add structure to creativity.

10 - Should you fire your best friend?

This is an interesting dilemma to discuss with your kid.

Pretend you hired your best friend, Mary, to help you with your venture. Mary enjoys working and loves the money you are paying to her. The problem is that Mary is not really doing a good job. Some of your customers are complaining about her laziness, and you now face a dilemma.

Should you fire your best friend or spend a lot of effort training her while trying to improve her motivation?

11 - Solving your grandparent's problems.

Problems are great opportunities to start new ventures. A problem means that there's possibly a customer willing to pay money for your solution. The solution may either be a product or a service.

Tell your kid to focus on their grandparents and the challenges they face. This is a useful exercise in empathy, out-of-the-box thinking, and how to develop ideas, or brainstorm. Here's how to set it up:

- Write "large problems," "small problems," "frequent problems," and "infrequent problems" in four columns.

- Then, start asking probing questions to help your kid identify problems. What does their day look like? What are their struggles? What type of help do they need?

- When you have written ten or more problems on the paper, go into problem-solving mode to tackle each problem with the following questions: Is the solution to the problem a product or a service? Is the solution something a kid can create and deliver on? Will your grandparents pay for the solution?

Write the answer to each of these questions on the paper next to each problem. Next time you visit with your grandparents, bring the results from this exercise along and discuss the problems and solutions. Do they agree, or do they point out important problems you may have missed?

12 - What is a good logo?

Logos are everywhere and come in all types, sizes, and shapes. Discussing logos is fun and gets your creative juices flowing. When driving, check out the logos you spot on buildings, signs, or other vehicles, or flip through a newspaper or magazine. In your discussions, here are a few points to consider:

- *Simplicity and Readability* – Some of the world's best logos, like Coca-Cola, are easy to read and simplistic in form. When looking at logos from small local companies, you might see that many are overly complicated and sometimes difficult to read.

- *Fonts* – Do you like the fonts used in the logo? When you look at logos side-by-side, it's interesting to talk about why companies made their choices. If you keep two logos the same but switch fonts, will you still have the same feeling when you look at the logo?

- *Colors* – Different colors trigger different emotions. Blue is a conservative color often used by insurance companies and financial companies, while other colors are more playful. Ask your kid why they think the company chose their logo color? If the color is changed to orange, would you take the company seriously?

- *Symbol* – Many logos have a symbol, like Nike and Starbucks. Examine logos with and without symbols and ask what your kid prefers?

Some logos have hidden meanings. Look up these logos online and have fun examining them together:

- *FedEx* – They are a transportation company. Check if you can see the hidden arrow in the letters.
- *Toyota* – Can you see that their symbol incorporates all the letters in the word "Toyota"?
- *Pinterest* – Can you see that there is something funny going on with the "P"?
- *Toblerone* – Can you see the bear hiding in the mountain image?
- *Amazon* – What is going on with the arrow? It looks like something, and what does it point from and to within the word "amazon"?
- *The Bronx Zoo* – Can you see the buildings between the giraffes' legs?

13 - What is the best business idea - homework tutor or gaming teacher?

Ask your kid what business they would start; become a tutor helping kids with homework or being a gaming teacher for kids to take their skills to the next level.

Kids of all ages need help with their homework, and parents are willing to pay for it. You can start a tutoring business where you meet with kids one-on-one in person or online and help them with their math lessons or other classes.

Kids love computer games but few have great skills. You can help kids in the neighborhood by coaching them one-on-one in video games. They will quickly improve their skills and soon master popular games. Here are a few questions to probe the reasoning of your kid's decision:

- Which business is the most fun to start?
- Where would you make the most money?
- What is the easiest to start?
- Do these businesses have the same customers?
- For the business you like the best: How would you set up your business? What would be your prices? Which customers would you sell to? How would you do the marketing? Would you make a website? What will it take for your kid to start this business next weekend?

14 - Watch Jerry Maguire with your kid.

Jerry Maguire is a great movie to watch with older kids. It has many lessons to discuss for life and business. Here are some of the takeaways from the movie to talk about afterward:

- *A leap of faith* – Many entrepreneurs like Jerry must make a leap of faith into something new. Life is too short to keep doing something you don't love or that's not aligned with your values (but make sure to tell them they still need to do their homework for a few more years).

- *Success doesn't come overnight and takes hard work* – In life, and for Jerry, success takes time and requires a lot of setbacks and hard work. Talk about your kid's passions and what it may take to reach their life goal.

- *Work is more than just earning money* – Focusing too much on the money you make doesn't bring happiness to your life.

- *Relationships* – Solid relationships are essential in business and life. Build and maintain relationships with everyone you meet, and it will serve you well in the future.

15 - Is creating a meal kit for kids to cook a good idea?

Ask your kid if they think it's a good idea to start a venture selling meal kits for kids in grocery stores. These kits include a kid-friendly recipe and are filled with all the ingredients a kid needs to make dinner for their family. You can set up a small factory to produce these meal kits, and then sell them to supermarkets for customers to purchase.

- What is the biggest challenge with this business?
- How many meal kits do you think you could sell in a month?
- If you start this venture, do you think it will be successful?

16 - Play the game Rollercoaster Tycoon.

Rollercoaster Tycoon is a series of computer games that will inspire creativity and teach you business skills. The game can be played on various platforms, including your smartphone.

In the game, the players build and operate their own theme parks with endless creative possibilities, business and game limitations, and lots of fun.

Playing this game with your kid will teach them lots of valuable skills like planning, building, maintaining, and keeping an eye on operational cost and customer satisfaction through a theme park business model.

17 - To-do lists for kids.

To-do lists are an essential tool for business and life tasks for many adults.

On the weekend, over breakfast, discuss the concept with your kid.

Then, ask your kid to make a list of the day's activities with checkboxes beside each item.

Have your kid keep it with them throughout the day and check off completed activities as the day progresses.

At night before going to bed, look at the list and see how many activities were completed. If many activities are unchecked, you can discuss if the plan was too ambitious.

On the other hand, if all items were competed should your kid have set higher goals?

18 - Understanding cost and margin.

This is a fun activity you can do many times and it may even become a ritual between you and your kid.

Start with a product in front of you. It can be anything—a sandwich, a soda, a pair of jeans, a smartphone, a table, and so on.

You then ask your kid, "How much do you think it costs to produce it?"

There are many ways to approach this question. The purpose is not to guess a number but to use reason to predict the cost. One way to approach the cost is to split the product into raw materials, labor costs, other costs, and profits. Finally, you have the cost of selling it and sales tax:

- *Raw material* – This is all the ingredients, parts, or materials that go into making the product. Identifying the ingredients and/or parts is a fun exercise. With your list of ingredients, discuss how much each could cost. Don't spend too much time trying to guess exact prices. You could look up the ingredients' prices online. For instance, if you identify plastic as part of the product and estimate that it weighs a kilo, you can search to find the price of a kilo of plastic.

- *Labor and other costs* – Ingredients and raw materials are not all that goes into a product. It also includes how the product is produced. If you both agree that the product is made by hand (or manual work), you'll have to estimate how long it takes to make it and the cost per hour. Remember, when discussing the cost per hour, you can add difficulty by including social costs, etc., which drives up the company's cost. Is the product made by a machine or in combination with humans? Examine the product for clues. If it's made of plastic, can you see the points where the plastic has been injected by a machine? If machines produced it, the production cost is usually low. But a factory has more expenses than just running the machines. It has managers, accounting, sales, and marketing departments, etc. These additional expenses are sometimes referred to as "overhead costs" and can often be higher than the actual production cost.
- *Profit* – The producer is in the business of making money and have a profit that adds to the product.
- *Cost of selling* – If you bought the product in a store, that store would have a margin on selling it. The margin can be between 20% to 70% depending on the type of store and product. Thinking of margins can be complicated, so many prefer to think in multiples. Most stores work with a multiple between two and four, which means that if they buy the product from a supplier for $100, they sell it for $200 to $400.
- *Sales tax* – In most markets, there is a sales tax adding to the product's cost. Discuss with your kid what sales tax is and why it exists. Sales tax exists because it generates a lot of income to the state; it's a consumption tax, not a tax on work, and equal for all, and it's immune to tax-avoiding schemes.

19 - Develop crazy ideas

For some entrepreneurs, the recipe for coming up with a good idea is to develop lots of ideas, even crazy ideas.

In this exercise, the objective is to come up with as many crazy ideas as possible. The crazier, the better.

At the same time, all the ideas should be commercial, meaning that they should have a price and a customer in mind.

Some thought starters:

- What is the wildest idea you have for products to be sold to kids at school?
- What is the craziest idea for a service you can offer to families in the neighborhood?
- What is the wildest idea you have for a YouTube channel?
- What is the craziest idea you have for something to be sold to the government to better the environment?

20 - What is your movie popcorn?

Discuss movie popcorn with your kid.

What makes it so unique? From a business standpoint, the most amazing thing about this special "type" of popcorn is that it's very cheap to produce, but very expensive for customers to buy. Amazingly it still sells in large quantities.

Ask your kid about what they think makes movie popcorn so special that theaters can charge such high prices at the concession stand (there is lots of melted butter on the popcorn; it is sold in huge buckets; you can only buy it when you go to the theater, etc.).

This type of product is known as a high-margin product. Can you think of other high-margin products? Some examples are:

- Clothes
- Computer software
- Food in restaurants
- Coffee and tea

Ask your kid what is their "movie popcorn"—in other words, what could they buy for cheap and sell for top dollars?

21 - Build the theme park of your dreams.

Are you ready for a fun adventure together?

What about planning, building, and running an imaginary theme park?

This adventure will take anywhere from two hours to two days. You should try to go through each step below, and the more time you spend on each step, the more fun and interesting this activity will be.

You can write it all down or just keep the discussion in your head, but keep in mind you will revisit many of these steps:

Step 1: The theme of the theme park – What type of amusement park does your kid want to create? Start with the activities, characters, and movies they love; should they make a theme park based upon a favorite computer game (Fortnite, Minecraft, etc.); a TV series they enjoy (Flash, Paw Patrol, Star Wars, etc.); or a magical book series (Harry Potter, The Hunger Games, etc.)? The theme can be unreal. Some aspects of this exercise do not have to be grounded in reality.

Step 2: Major attractions – Have your kid describe some of the major attractions in the theme park. Here they can test their wild imagination. The wilder, the better. If you have time, have your kid draw some of the attractions. It may further stimulate their creativity. You might bring in some engineering limitations to make it more realistic, but wild is fun at this stage of the planning process.

Step 3: Location – The park needs a location. Where does your kid want to place the park? Here is a chance to discuss the trade-off between a location downtown or one outside the city. Once you have decided on a location, everything gets more real.

Step 4: The market and customers – Who is the customer? If the theme is narrow, the park will receive fewer visitors than one with a broader theme. Based on your kid's theme and location of choice, you can then discuss the potential market. How many people live within a one-hour radius of the theme park? How often will they visit during a season?

Step 5: Competitors and substitutes – A company should know its competitors and what they offer, their strengths and weaknesses, and how they price their offerings.

Direct competitors offer a similar product and service. For an amusement park, direct competitors are other amusement parks or other types of play parks. Discuss how they are similar and different.

There are also substitutes, or an offering that fulfills the same need but is not an amusement park. Substitutes may be anything that customers can spend their money on instead of spending it in an amusement park. If your kid decides that their customers are families, then an indirect competitor of their theme park may be bowling alleys, movie theaters, go-kart tracks, etc.

Step 6: Marketing – How would you do the marketing for your customers to become aware of the new park?

For this exercise, you can separate the discussion into two parts: The channel and the message.

Start with the channel. Here you discuss the media channels that best reach your target customers. Would you use ads on TV, billboards, Facebook, Instagram, newspapers, radio, or others? Ask your kid, "why?" and have an interesting discussion on which channel they think would be best for their customers.

Then it's on to the message. How would you communicate the new theme park? Should you focus on the rides, the customers' experience, the price, or other aspects? If you have time, let your kid draw some advertisements. Have them look at competitors' advertisements for inspiration.

Step 7: The economics – Now on to the numbers. Here you should get out a pen and paper. Start by calculating the income, or revenue, of the park:

- The first thing your kid needs to decide on is the price of admission. Should there be a differentiated price for kids and adults, and do you have a VIP pass for customers who want to avoid waiting in lines? You can check out what competitors are charging by looking up their parks online. The guests will also buy food and drinks and souvenirs at the theme park., You should estimate a sum per visitor for each of these items, too.

- Then, estimate the number of customers who will visit the park on an average day. Try to reason and make a guess. To check your numbers, search online for guest numbers of other major theme parks.

Cost of personnel – You need to discuss how many people will work in the park and their average salary. Help your kid check the numbers. You then get the daily salary cost and multiply it by the number of days the park is open to get the total personnel cost.

Cost of food, drinks, and souvenirs – Previously, you estimated how much money each guest spends on food and drinks. It has a cost, and now you need to estimate it. The easiest way to calculate the cost is to let the cost be a percentage of the food and drink revenues, for example, 30%. So, if the revenues are $10, then the cost is $3.

Cost of land – As the park owner, you can either buy the land as an investment or rent the land. If you choose to buy it, you will need more money upfront. If you rent the space, you will pay a monthly rental fee. To make it easy for yourself, set the cost at 10% of the revenues of the park.

Cost of marketing – Advertising the park costs money. Discuss how much money to spend on ads. A good rule of thumb would be somewhere between 3% and 10%.

Cost of rides – You will either invest in building your own rides or rent the rides from a supplier. For this exercise, you should assume that you rent the rides, and it costs you 15% of revenues.

Miscellaneous costs – All businesses have other costs—some are expected, and some are not. Discuss with your kids what these costs might be (accountants, electricity bills, lawyer fees, etc.) Give this cost a percentage, somewhere between 2% and 5%.

Step 8: Should you start this business? – Now that you have the whole picture.

- What does your kid think of the plans? Is he/she excited?
- Is it an interesting business? Why?
- Will it make money? Why?
- Finally, what do you think? Should you quit your day job and help your kid launch this amusement park in real life ?

22 - Invest with your kids.

Investing in companies will teach your kids many valuable business lessons.

You may either buy the stock/commodity or pretend to buy it as listed in the examples below. If you pretend, keep the purchase price and the number of stocks in a spreadsheet for recordkeeping.

Here are a few interesting ways to introduce your kid to investing:

- Sometimes the number of stocks available to invest in can be overwhelming. Instead, give your kid one hour to research two different stocks of your choosing. Show them a few online sites where they can do the research; then, based on their recommendation, buy the stock. After four weeks, check the performance of the two stocks. If their stock choice performed better than the one you did not buy, give them a price, or reward, possibly the value of the stock.

- Pick up a financial newspaper and read it with your kids. Based on the companies in the paper, they get to select one stock. Give the stock four weeks, and if the stock has increased in value after that time, let your kid keep the increase.

- Let your kid choose any stock on the market. Note down the price. If the stock increases in value over the next month, give them the increase.

- Tell your kid they can invest in either gold or Bitcoin. Note down the value of both items on the day they make their choice. Give the investment a few weeks, and if their choice performed better than the other item, give them a reward, possibly ice cream.

- You can also make money when stocks fall in value. This is called to "short" a stock. Let your kid select any stock to short. They get a reward if the stock actually falls in value.

The most important activity for all these investment exercises is the discussion before buying the stock and the reflection after seeing its fluctuation in value. Can your kid explain why the stock fell or increased in value?

23 - Business Sunday: Launch a waffle and lemonade stand before lunch.

A waffle and lemonade stand is one of the classic businesses a kid can start. It's quite easy to set up and a great learning experience for both of you. Here's how to do it:

Step 1: Deciding on what to sell – A fundamental first step is to decide on what items to sell at your stand. In making the decision, you have to consider many factors:

- *What does your kid enjoy cooking?* It will not be a fun experience if he/she hates eating or drinking what foods they make.

- *What do customers want to buy?* There is no use offering something that customers don't want to purchase. Cotton candy is fun to make, but sales will be minuscule if only adults and seniors pass by the stand.

- *What can you make money on?* Some food and drink items have good margins, while others are difficult to sell with a profit. Selling sodas and candy are examples since it's readily available in stores with established price points.

When you have decided on your primary offering, like waffles, it might be a good idea to select some complimentary products to sell, like lemonade, coffee, etc.

Step 2: Deciding on where to sell it – To succeed with selling from a stand, you need to be located at a place where there is a lot of foot traffic passing by. It will make it more fun, and your kid will be better able to sell and market the offering. Remember, if a power cord is needed to make waffles, coffee, etc., it may restrict where you can set up shop.

Step 3: Setting the prices – Setting prices can either be a one-minute or a one-hour exercise. You will create the best learning experience by first estimating the cost per unit you sell. If you are selling waffles, you calculate the cost of ingredients (you can look up the prices online) and then divide it by the number of waffles the recipe makes. You can do the calculation in a spreadsheet or on paper. Let your kid complete the calculations while you help them when needed. Consider adding the cost of your child's time to the cost per unit (waffle). Asking them about their cost per hour can lead to all kinds of interesting discussions. After you calculate your baseline cost per unit, look at competitors' prices for similar products. Finally, consider if there are some psychological price points you can utilize. Pricing a product at $10.50 is not optimal. See if you can sell it at $9.90 or $14.90. The last point to consider when it comes to pricing is if you are going to have some combination of offers, like *two waffles for xx, or waffles and lemonade for yy*.

Step 4: Making the poster – Making a poster will force your child to make many decisions. What is the name of the venture, and will it have a logo? If it does, then you draw it on the poster. Will the products have more descriptive names, like "super waffles"? On the poster, you should also write the price of each product. Discuss if the poster should have a headline to draw the attention of people passing by. Should you use different colors, large letters, or employ other tricks to get people to notice the poster?

Step 5: Making the food – Have a discussion about how much food and drink to make at the stand. What is the plan if all of the items sell out, and what happens if nothing is sold? Make sure the food is made hygienically.

Step 6: Selling the food – Now it's time to set up the stand. Hang the poster up and start selling. You should become a customer and get others to stop by, too.

Starting a venture is no dance on roses, and some struggle is an essential part of any start-up business. Have your kid track some data while they are selling at the stand. How many people pass by? How many people notice the poster? How many stop? And how many people become customers? All this data can be interesting to discuss later.

Step 7: Counting the money and evaluating – Time to pack up and get home to evaluate. Some questions to discuss:

- How many units of the different products were sold?
- How much money did you make? If you subtract the cost of the products you had to throw away, did you make money?
- What part was the most fun?
- What would you like to change?
- Should we do it again the next weekend?

24 - What is the best idea - a slime factory or a bath bomb factory?

Ask your kid what business they would like to choose between starting a slime factory producing all types of slime or a bath bomb factory, making round dissolving bath salts.

In your slime factory, you make slime of all types and sizes. It's then put into boxes and sold to kids at school or in the local community.

Many kids enjoy bath bombs that quickly dissolve when placed into bathwater. In your factory, you produce bath bombs with different smells, colors, and sizes.

Here are a few questions to probe their reasoning:

- Which business is the most fun to start?
- Where would you make the most money?
- What business is the easiest to start?
- Do these businesses have the same customers or are they different?
- For the business, you like the best: How would you set up the business? What would be your prices? Which customers would you sell to? How would you do the marketing? Would you make a website?

What will it take for your kid to start this business next weekend?

25 - What is cross-selling?

Can you go one month without giving way to cross-selling techniques? Probably not.

Ask your kid if he/she knows about cross-selling. Most likely, they will say "no," but you and your kid have experienced it many, many times.

"Would you like batteries with the electronic toy?" "Do you want a pair of matching socks to go with the pants?" These are both examples of cross-selling, which means selling you more products than what you had originally planned to buy. The objective of cross-selling is to increase your basket size. As everyone familiar with retail knows, it's always easier to sell more products to existing customers than to bring new customers into the store.

Bring your kid along to local stores to see if the product placement on the shelves attempts to cross-sell. Visit online stores and put products into the shopping basket and see if other products are recommended.

Online companies try to cross-sell to you for example by pop-ups or: "Customers who buy this also buy this…"

If your kid is experimenting with some businesses of their own. Have them think about cross-selling opportunities.

26 - Watch infomercials together

Infomercials have inspired many entrepreneurs.

They are long-form TV advertisements where a product or service is sold to the viewer in a spot ranging from thirty seconds to thirty minutes.

Some TV channels show infomercials early in the morning or late at night. There are even channels devoted to infomercials and at-home shopping, like QVC. If you can't watch them live, you can search for infomercials on YouTube.

Watch a few infomercials together with your kid to see what you may learn from their selling techniques. Here are points to discuss with your kid after viewing:

- What do the infomercials have in common, and why have they structured the ads in the way they have?
- All infomercials have elements of demonstration. What can you learn from how the products are demonstrated?
- Most of these advertisements use testimonials from customers. Why are they letting customers do the selling and not the company themselves?
- The main points and offers are repeated in infomercials. Since TV airtime is expensive, would it not be better to say things only once? Why or why not?

- USP stands for unique selling points and is the main reason why anyone should buy the product. What are the arguments, and how are they structured in the ad?
- What is the offer, and what does the company or host do to convince you that it's of great value? A classical trick is to show you before and after prices, or that the value of each element is costly when bought individually, but the bundle is a good offer.
- Is the host doing anything to create scarcity? *Scarcity* means you create a sense of urgency for the customer to take action. The company usually provokes scarcity with time limitations (today only), product limitations (limited stock), and so on. See if you can spot their marketing tricks.
- Has the company or host created offers that include upsells (offer you an upgrade to a more expensive product) or cross-sells (selling you more items in addition to their primary offer)?
- Is free shipping included? If "yes," why do you think they are offering it?
- Does the company provide any guarantees, like money back, etc.? Guarantees cost money. The question you should ask yourself is if it's worth it.

27 - Is starting a temp agency for kids a good idea?

Ask your kid if they think it's a good idea to start a temp agency.

This agency would ask other kids to register for local work opportunities, and your kid assigns the employees to customers in the neighborhood who need help with babysitting, lawn mowing, house cleaning, and so on.

Your kid essentially coordinates the work, collects payments, and pays the employees. Your kid would charge the customers more than they pay the kids working, and your kid makes money off others work.

Ask your kid:

- What is the largest challenge with this business?
- How much would it be possible to sell in a month?
- If you were to start this venture, do you think it would be successful?

28 - Brainstorming with your kids.

Brainstorming is a powerful tool to develop lots of ideas quickly.

Bring your kids along for fun.

First, you have to pick a topic for the brainstorming. Some examples are; *activities to do on a Saturday, gifts to buy for Mom's birthday, cool new dinner recipes, etc.* Use your creativity to come up with more brainstorming topic ideas.

- Dedicate thirty to sixty minutes for the brainstorming and turn off all smartphones.
- Ideally, your group should be from three to six people.
- Get a bunch of Post-it notes in different colors.
- Spend five minutes working independently in silence to jot down all your ideas—one idea per Post-it note.
- Then, circle around the group and pick a note from each participant. Read it aloud and stick each one on the wall.
- When all the ideas from the individual brainstorming are on the wall, you are ready for new ideas. When seeing others' ideas, it's usually easier to come up with even more new ideas.
- Whenever there's a new idea, have the person that came up with it write it down and stick it on the wall.

- In this process, it's essential not to be critical, giggle out loud, etc. Explain that the purpose of the brainstorm is to have ideas flow freely and not have skeptics stop the ideation process.
- When the ideas are drying up, stop. Take a photograph of the wall to document the event.
- The brainstorming session has now ended. You can call it a day or start sorting the ideas. If you sort the ideas right away, use the Post-it notes to sort the ideas on the wall into different categories like *great ideas, good ideas, unrealistic, and bad ideas.* Take another photo to document these categories before recycling the sticky notes.
- Then, prioritize and decide what to do with the *best and good ideas*. Save the *unrealistic and bad ideas* just for reference.

29 - Raising 1,000 dollars to start a new venture.

Some ventures require money to get off the ground. To set up this activity, tell your kid they have this fantastic idea for an exciting new venture selling ice cream, but they need to raise or obtain 1,000 dollars to make it happen. How would they raise the money?

Start with "who." Who would they talk to, and why would they be a good resource? You can have a good discussion on who they know that could be interested in either making a good investment or who believes in his/her ability to succeed.

Then, on to the "how":

- How would they present their venture idea and ask for the money?
- Would they make a slideshow presentation, or just talk to the potential investor?
- What would they emphasize, and would they offer something in return to the investor (only the money back, money back with interest or ownership in the new business)?

Along the way, discuss good persuasion techniques and how to appeal to your audience.

30 - Understanding price elasticity

Price elasticity.

It's such a difficult word, but such a cool concept, and is a great starting point for an interesting discussion with your kid. Here's how to set it up.

Take any product and ask your kid to guess the price and how many of that product is sold in a year. This is an interesting exercise in reasoning, but not the main point here.

You then ask, "what would happen to the sales if the price was doubled?" Your kid will most likely say that the volume will be reduced as customers may decide on products from competitors or substitutes (or products that solve similar problems for the customer).

Then, you ask what will happen if the price is cut in half. In most instances, the sales will go up.

You now have three price points: the original price and sales volume, the doubled price with a new volume, and the halved price and new volume. You could put this into a graph with price on the Y-axis and units on the X-axis. If you draw the line, you will see that volumes increase when the price is reduced.

How the sales volume changes when prices change is called *price elasticity*. Some products are sensitive to small changes in price, and some are not.

As your kids now understand the concept, you can ask them what happens to the volume of these products if the price is cut in half or doubled:

- Nike running shoes
- Toilet paper
- Popcorn in movie theaters
- Milk
- Legos

A fun counterintuitive point to this general principle is fashion, where sales might go up when prices increase since it may signal quality, design and luxury. Another example is a toothbrush. If a company decides to increase the purchase price to become the most expensive toothbrush available, some customers may think this is the best brush on the market, leading to increased demand.

31 - Solving your parent's problems?

Problems are great opportunities to start new ventures. A problem means that there's possibly a customer willing to pay money for your solution. The solution may either be a product or a service. Tell your kid to focus on their parent's challenges.

This is a useful exercise in empathy, out-of-the-box thinking, and how to develop ideas. Here's how to set it up:

- Write "large problems," "small problems," "frequent problems," and "infrequent problems" in four columns on a sheet of paper.

- Then start asking probing questions to help your kid identify problems. What does their mom's day look like? What are her struggles? What help does she need?

- When you are finished with problems, go into problem-solving mode to tackle each problem with the following questions: Is the solution to the problem a product or a service? Is the solution something a kid can create or deliver on? Will your parents pay for the solution?

Write the answer to each of these questions on the paper next to the problem. Since you are a parent, tell them how accurate they are in their identification of your problems and whether or not the solutions they come up with are of interest to you. What problems did they miss, and why?

32 - What questions to ask when hiring?

To begin, tell your kid, "You have started a business, and ten kids apply for a job working for you. What interview questions do you ask them?"

This is a fun and interesting exercise. It gets to the core of one of the important skills of any company: hiring. It will make the both of you reflect and learn something new. Here are some elements to discuss and questions to ask in an interview:

- *Competence or background* - Where have you learned the skills we are looking for in this role? Have you had similar jobs before? Give the applicant a test so they can show you their skills.

- *Personality* - What are your strengths and weaknesses? How would you describe yourself as a person? How do others describe you?

- *Fit with you and the company* - Why are you motivated for this job? What types of colleagues do you like to work with?

- *More in-depth questions* - Brain teasers like how many chocolate bars do kids at school eat in a year? Why should we hire you? What question do you wish we would ask? Give examples of times you have messed up at work and how you handled it?

33 - Understanding scale advantages.

At the onset of the company, why did Tesla sell their cars for a lower price than what it cost to produce?

This is a good starting point for a fun discussion. When talking about this topic, you should have a pen and paper nearby.

After reasoning a little about how stupid Elon Musk must have been to initially sell cars at a loss, ask your kid how much money they think it would cost to produce just one of many different products you can come up with, and then how much would it cost to make a thousand, and then a million units of that product.

Is it more expensive per product to produce less or more?

The answer is that the more products you produce, the lower your cost. The effect has many names, including scale advantage.

Now it's time to bring out your pen and paper. Draw a horizontal line and write "units" on it. Then, draw a vertical line at the left end (so you have a graph) and write "cost."

If you only produce one item, ask your kid if the price is high or low. Draw a point close to the vertical line high up, illustrating high-cost with a low volume.

Then move further out on the horizontal line and ask what happens to the cost of the product with a volume of 1,000, and so on. With a few points in the graph, you can now draw a line. This shows how cost decreases as volume increases.

Elon Musk knew that if Tesla increased sales volume for their cars, the production cost would go down until they started to make money.

Your kid might ask why the cost is reduced when volume increases. Many factors can contribute to this, including:

- At higher volumes, you can use more efficient production methods, driving the cost down.
- Larger volumes require more raw material that you can buy at lower prices.
- At higher volumes, you can invest in robot machinery for even more efficient production lines.
- As you produce more of the product, the organization learns best practices, which leads to greater efficiency and lower costs.

34 - The elevator pitch.

In business, there is a concept called the elevator pitch.

The objective of the pitch is to explain your business so clearly that you can convince a shareholder to invest in your company in the amount of time it takes to ride an elevator—about thirty seconds.

Learning to summarize and clearly explain a topic is a valuable skill in life and business.

Whenever you are riding an elevator with your kids, ask them before entering to present a topic. It can be any topic of interest from school, family to movies and games.

The time restraint of the short elevator ride adds pressure to the situation.

After you do this exercise several times, you will see your kid improve in structuring their thinking and will be able to present more clearly and concisely each time they practice.

35 - Let your kid be your manager.

What does it take to be a manager or a leader? This is difficult to know, even for adults. You can give your kids some leadership and management training that is fun and exciting for both of you. Here are some examples:

- *Manager of the dinner* – Give your kid a budget and let him/her plan the dinner. They then have to make the grocery shopping list and ask a person in the family to do the shopping. The kid is not allowed to do the shopping or any food preparation but instead has to delegate tasks, coordinate the timing and make sure everyone completes their task correctly. Who will cut the vegetables, fry the fish, set the table, light the candles, and so on? It's a fun exercise allowing your kid to practice planning, splitting a large task into smaller items, delegating, and following up with other people.

- *Manage to get to school on time* – The night before a school day, agree with your kid that they will be in charge of the morning routine. They set the time for the alarm clock. When it rings, he/she wakes up their family members and delegates the tasks for the family to have a good morning. Who should make breakfast? Do people spend too much time to get dressed? And who is making lunch for school and work? It's a high-pressure situation due to the deadline, but may be fun and provide lessons.

Manage a Saturday – Let your kid be in charge of a Saturday. On Friday night, start to brainstorm what they want to do and their initial plan for the day after. The plan should include activities from when the family wakes up until they go to bed. Your kid is fully in charge of what the family does for the entire day.

- Who makes breakfast? Who sets the table? Who is responsible for cleaning up afterward?
- Plan and arrange activities to do together.
- What is for dinner? Who does the grocery shopping? Who prepares the food?
- What are other decisions your kid has to make and delegate for your family's needs?

36 - Can you improve the TV ad?

When watching TV or YouTube with your kid, pay special attention to the advertisements.

Rotate who "gets" to comment on the commercial. Pause the video after you watch the commercial, and the person who "owns" the commercial comments on it and suggests improvements. Some questions to provoke comments are:

- Which type of customer does the ad target?
- What is sold, and what are the USPs (unique selling points to convince you to buy the product)?
- What would you change about the ad?
- Did you like the actors or would you choose different ones?
- Would you do something completely different to market the product?

37 - Is creating a homemade strawberry and raspberry jam a great idea?

Ask your kid if they think it's a good idea to start a venture selling their own jam.

The jam could be a combination of strawberry and raspberry flavor and comes in a glass jar with a professional label.

The jam could sold in your neighborhood, from a stand, or at farmer's markets. After explaining the concept, discuss:

- What is the largest challenge with this business?
- How much jam would be possible to sell in a month?
- How much money might you make?
- If you were to start this venture, do you think it would be successful?

38 - How do Netflix and Spotify make money?

Open the websites or apps from Netflix and Spotify and ask your kid how they believe these companies make money.

It's a fun and exciting exercise that will help your kid understand more about companies with newer business models. Play around on the website to see if your kid figures out the companies' business model:

- The revenues from these companies are primarily from subscriptions. Check out the prices of their different subscriptions. Can you see a difference between the two services? Spotify has a free version where you get to listen to music with commercial breaks. Advertisers pay for the commercials and this becomes revenue for Spotify. Netflix has only paid subscriptions. Would it make sense for Netflix to also have a free offer?

- Ask your kid what type of costs these companies have. Both have the cost of acquiring content from other sources. Discuss how the company pays for it. Do you think they buy the content rights forever, for a certain time period, or pay-per-view (the answer is that Netflix pays to have the content for a period of time in a market, while Spotify pays based on the number of artists streams.) Netflix also produces their own content, and Spotify does not.

In addition to the cost of content, these companies have the cost of their employees, technology, advertising, rent, etc.

Other cool things to discuss:

- What happens if there's a price increase or a price decrease of the subscription?
- If you were starting a competing streaming service, how would your offerings be different?
- Do you have any ideas to start a venture with the same business model as Netflix?

39 - What is his/her occupation?

When you are sitting together with your kid in a restaurant or on public transportation, play a game where you guess what the people around you do for a living.

It's a fun and surprisingly insightful game. Why insightful, might you ask?

Because the choice of occupation has consequences, and certain people are drawn toward specific careers.

If ten people suround you on the bus, can you spot the teacher, the lawyer, the engineer, or is it be impossible to identify a person's job?

When you play the game, you will soon figure out some clues for your guesses.

- What does a man wearing a suit say about his occupation?
- If someone has a big tattoo, does this influence where the person works?
- Can eyeglasses, shopping bags, shoes, or work uniforms give you any clues?
- Try not to fall into obvious stereotype traps and instead look for logical context clues to inform your decision. Keep in mind that this game's lessons might impact your kids' choice of studies and careers in the future.

40 - The idea journal

Ideas foster ideas.

The more you train your creative muscles, the stronger they get.

Buy your kid a cool notebook with the aim to come up with 365 business ideas in a year. Let your kid be creative and remind her/him to work on the journal ideas at least once a week. Discuss the business ideas in their journal before putting your kid to bed.

If their fountain of creativity runs dry, come up with some thought-provoking questions to get it flowing again.

41 - What is a good brand name?

Company names come in all forms and shapes. When driving, walking in a city or reading a magazine, you will see hundreds of company names. Use this as an arena to play a fun game with your kid by asking:

- What are the coolest and worst names you see and why? The purpose is not what names you choose, but the discussion on what makes it good and exciting.

- What do you think the company does? If you see a new or a strange name, can you guess the company's business based on the name and logo? After you both have made a guess, you can check it online.

Here are points to use in discussing the qualities of names:

- Some names describe what the company does, like *The Painter, Computer Help*, etc. Do you like these types of names the best? Why or why not?

- Some names describe what the customer gets in return from the company or product: *Relief pills, Relaxation pillows*, etc. Do you like these types of names?

- Do you like companies named after their founders?

- Some names are made up. Spotify is an example of this type of name. Having a made-up name makes it easier to purchase domain names and to protect the use of the name in copyrights.

42 - Should you invest in a company with a cool product?

Initiate an exciting conversation based on a cool product that your kid has or wants. By linking the discussion to something they desire, it will make the talk more memorable and easier for them to grasp.

If your kid plays video games, likes smartphones, dolls, or a certain brand of clothes, use those as examples for this exercise.

Say, "I know you want a new Apple iPhone, but do you think owning a part of the company is a good idea, too?" Here are some points to bring up:

- *Do you think existing investors in the company also believe the product is cool?* Your kid loves a product, but so do other people, and it may already reflected in the stock price. Look up the stock price of the company together with your kid. Ideally, they do the search. Check to see if you can find out the P/E number. The "E" stands for earnings and was the company's profit last year. The "P" stands for the company price. By dividing the "P" with the "E," you can see how many years will pass with last year's profit to make up the price of the company. If the P/E is 10, the investors value the company at ten times last year's profit. A high P/E means people expect great things from the company in the future.

- *Is it better to own a company with a cool product than to own one with a boring one?* This discussion can be had at many levels. What is the purpose of owning a company or a stock in the company? If it is just to make money, it doesn't matter if the company has a cool product. If the product is cool, it will most likely have made the stock more expensive to buy. A boring company with boring products can make lots of money and be a better investment than a cool company with cool products that investors already love.

43 - Who in your class would you hire for help?

Tell your kid they are starting a business and that they need to hire someone from their class to work with them.

If they have to hire a classmate to help them make waffles, who would they hire? What makes that person the ideal candidate for the job? How would they train the person to become a great waffle maker?

On the other hand, if they need to find someone in their class to help them make a YouTube channel, who would they hire? What makes that person the ideal candidate for the job, and how would you work together?

If they need to hire someone from their class to sell the products they are making (like bath soaps or jam), who would they want? What makes that person the ideal candidate for the job, and how would they work together?

44 - Watch Dragon's Den and Shark Tank together.

Dragon's Den and Shark Tank have become popular TV shows, and you will find many of the episodes on YouTube.

They have a high production value, and it's entertaining for young and old viewers alike. If you haven't watched them before, start by searching for "Shark Tank highlights" or "best of Dragon's Den" to get your kid excited about the show.

When your kid is hooked on these Tv shows, you can watch entire episodes where some of the pitches get a thumbs up, while others a thumbs down.

It may be even more exciting if you give yourself and your kid $100,000 in Monopoly money. After every sales pitch on the show, the two of you discuss and decide whether to invest in the company and how much money to invest. To maximize the lessons from this exercise, pause after each pitch and discuss the following:

- How did you like the idea? Judging ideas are never easy. Remember, many of the professional investors in these programs have turned down companies that became very successful afterwards. Would the idea work in your local market, and would you be willing to quit your job and your kid leave school to launch a similar venture?

- What did you think of the pitch and presentation? Could you have done it better, and how would you do it?
- Did the company valuation make sense, or were they too optimistic?
- Do you remember the questions asked by the investors? Why do you think they asked the questions they did?
- Was the company treated fairly on the show? Why or why not?

45 - Start a business on a car trip.

A car trip is a perfect opportunity to teach your kid about business. If the trip is about one hour, you will be able to help your kid start a business.

This is an entertaining exercise, and all you have to do is ask the right questions at the right time. Here's how to set it up:

- *The idea* – First, your kid needs to come up with an idea for a product or business. When coming up with ideas, it's often easier if you create some boundaries instead of being completely open in the brainstorming. Here are some ideas to get your kids thinking: "You have to come up with the idea for the Christmas present of the year." "What product will make your friends' lives better?" "You have to develop a new piece of clothing. What is it?" "Create a new product to use in the kitchen." It may be better for the exercise if the idea is for a concrete product instead of a computer game, app, etc.

- *The cost of the product* – Reasoning about the cost of producing the product is interesting. What are the raw materials included to make the product? How is the product made? You can bring up the cost of the manual labor going into making the product. If you have time, discuss how the costs change if you produce the product in another country compared to locally.

- *The customer and market* – Who is the customer of the product? Here you may discuss the age group, sex, and other characteristics of the target customer. If your kid likes math, try to calculate how large the potential market is for the product. If you focus on your country, then take the total population and divide it by 80 (the approximate life expectancy.) Let your kid do the calculation. Now you know the number of people who are ten years old, etc. If the customers you focus on are 10-14 years old, it spans over five years, and you multiply it by five. If your product is for girls only, you divide the number by two; and if it's for girls playing handball, you reduce it even further. The objective is not to get the math exactly right, but to practice reasoning skills.

- *The pricing of the product* – Getting the product pricing right is critical. The price should not be the same as your product cost because then you cannot cover other expenses and make a profit. If competitors are selling similar products, then those prices will be your guidelines. You also have to consider if others are going to sell the product for you. If you expect shops to sell your product at Christmas, then they need a margin. It may be easier to think of this in multiples. Most stores expect a multiple of between 2-3, which means they might buy the product for $10 and sell it for $20-$30. Discuss if you are going to use psychological pricing, for instance, setting the price at $99 instead of $100.

- *Marketing and selling the product* – Discuss with your kid how they would sell and market the product. When it comes to marketing, they can make posters, create brochures to drop in mailboxes, place advertisements in newspapers, magazines, or online. For selling, are you going to knock on doors, sell from a stand at the farmer's market, or do you have other ideas?
- *The budget* – Now your kid has the information they need to prepare a budget. Start with turnover (sales). Have him/her estimate the number of products they will sell and multiply it by the sales price they come up with.
- *The cost* – First, you calculate the product cost, which is the cost per unit multiplied by the number of units sold. If you are going to do sales and marketing, you have to spend some money on it. Discuss what level is reasonable. Then you have other costs like setting up an online store, the kid's salary, paying employees, etc.

Now you have thought through many of the important aspects of starting a business.

46 - Create your first budget

Understanding how to read and prepare budgets is a valuable skill in life and business. Budgeting can be taught to kids from a young age. Start by explaining the fundamentals:

- Everyone uses budgets. A family normally has a budget, a business definitely has one, and a country has many budgets. In other words, everyone around you has or uses budgets. They come in all variations:

  - Operational budgets show you the profit or loss of a business or household. This is the most common type of budget and the one you would make for a family.

  - While the operational budget tells you how much money you have (or don't have), it doesn't tell you if you are out of cash. The liquidity budget shows you exactly how much money you have at any given moment. It includes time as an important factor. For example, if you buy a sofa in January, it shows up in the operational budget in January, but if you pay for it with a credit card, you don't have to pay until March, and that's when it shows up in the liquidity budget.

  - Investment budgets are used to show the cost of entering into something new that will generate revenues and costs in the future.

- Project budgets have the revenues and cost of a single project. The project budget is often aggregated into operational budgets.
- Budgets can be made by-hand on paper or in a digital spreadsheet. Most budgets use very simple math, but the advantages of using a spreadsheet are that it quickly sums it all up and is easy to change.
- Your kid's first experience in making a budget may be to help you set up a yearly budget for the family. To help your kid see the value in a budget, make yours with pencil and paper:
- Start with the income. It includes your and a partner's salary, rents you receive if you are renting out a space, interest from your bank, etc. If there is more than one line of income, practice adding it together.
- Then you have the cost of the household. You don't have to be very detailed at this stage; instead focus on some of the larger elements. They may include: Rent or interest on a house loan. Cost of food, clothes, cost of technology (TV, laptop, cell phone), vacations. entertainment, etc.
- If you spend less than you make, explain that the rest of the money goes into a savings account.
- Then, have the kid type the budget into a spreadsheet. Use simple adding and subtraction formulas so they can see that changing one part of the budget automatically changes the sum.

Then your kid can make a budget for themselves. On the revenue/income side, they can have an allowance, gifts, etc. On the cost side, there will be clothes, toys, etc. Have your kids make a budget for a whole month and see if they can keep within the budget.

47 - How to handle all the cash.

Handling money is a challenge for all companies and kids starting ventures. It was easier before when coins and bills were the primary means of purchase rather than buying items with a smart phone or credit and debit cards. People still use cash. If the products or services are compelling enough, customers will find a way to pay you. If customers don't have cash on them, consider giving them credit and collect the cash later.

- Make sure all money is handled properly. Get a box for it, preferably with a lock. Avoid stuffing bills into your pockets, as it looks unprofessional. Don't keep too much money around the house, as it might be tempting for others to steal.

- In some markets, there are good alternative payment methods to transfer money peer-to-peer. In most instances, the transfer needs to be made from adult to adult, so consider having your kid's customers make payment to your bank account. Help your kid develop a system to track the funds they receive from their customers, and you pay them back to their account.

- If the venture becomes successful, and your kid is old enough, you should encourage her/him to open a bank account in their name. It will keep their money safe and growing.

48 - Create a new logo for Coca-Cola, Nike, and McDonald's.

These logos are among the world's most known.

Challenge your kid to make their own version of these companies' logos.

Print out the original logos for reference and let your kid experiment with drawing new ones on paper or a computer.

Discuss what the existing logos represents, why they are good, and how your kid's versions of the logos compare to the originals.

49 - Understanding USPs.

USPs are central to business and life in general. It stands for unique selling points. Products and people have USPs.

USPs answer the question, "Why choose us over our competitors?" When you become aware of them, you will see USPs all over the place. Here's how to teach USPs:

- Another kid is considering starting at your school. Why should they do it? What makes your school special? Have your kid list the USPs.
- Why should you start to watch your kid's favorite TV series? Can your kid convince you with the USPs of the series?
- What are the USPs of your smartphone? Is it the screen, battery life, performance, apps, etc.?
- If your kid is at a job interview, why should they be hired? Have them list their USPs.
- What are the USPs of the dinner you had yesterday? Is it healthy, tasty, large portions, unique sauce, etc.?

50: What is the best idea—become the neighborhood baker or candy maker?

Ask your kid what business they would like to start. A neighborhood baker serving rolls and bread on the weekends or being a candymaker mixing chocolates and hard candies. As the neighborhood baker, you get up early on weekends to bake bread and rolls. You then deliver the goods at the doors of your neighbors. Being a candy maker is a dream for many kids. You make candies and chocolates, wrap them, and sell them at school or locally. If the venture becomes a success, you can create a website to sell your tasty treats. Here are a few questions to probe the reasoning of your kid's decision:

- Which business do you think will be the most fun to start?
- Where would you make the most money?
- What is the easiest to start?
- Do these businesses have the same customers or are they different?
- For the business, you like the best: How would you do it? What would be your prices? Which customers would you sell to? How would you do the marketing? Would you make a website?

What will it take for your kid to start this business the next weekend?

51 - Teach your kid to set goals and achieve them.

Setting goals is a core skill in life and business.

Ask your kid to set three goals. It can be for anything: their sport, school, family life, etc. Teach your kids to set S.M.A.R.T goals.

S.M.A.R.T stands for:

- **S**pecific – A goal should be specific so it's easy to see if you achieve it or not.
- **M**easurable – To make sure a goal can be achieved, it needs an objective measure.
- **A**chievable – Unmet goals demotivate people. Make sure the goals can be achieved.
- **R**ealistic – Goals should be within reach and realistic to the person.
- **T**imely –The goal should have a start and end date.

Write the goals down on paper. Written goals are 80% more likely to be achieved,

Specifying the goal is an essential first step. Then, have your kids write down three actions to achieve each goal. Encourage your kid to go after the goal by completing the actions. When your kid succeeds in reaching the goal, mark it with a small celebration.

52 - Find problems we want solved and give us a price.

This exercise will teach your kid how to identify problems, set prices, and negotiate—all valuable business and life skills. Here's how to do this exercise:

- Tell your kid to look around the house to find problems or tasks that they believe you want to solve. This will teach your kids how to identify problems and have empathy for other's problems.
- Then he/she prepares an offer with a price to solve the problems for you. This will test their ability to set prices at the right level.
- Based on their offer, you can either accept the offer or negotiate. The negotiation will teach them valuable communication, cooperation and compromising skills.

53 - Is creating a homework station a good idea?

Ask your kid if they think it's a good idea to start a venture selling a homework station to kids who need to concentrate on their work. Your kid develops and designs a station with walls, a small roof, and a good writing surface for kids to use to complete their homework. You can add a good reading light, a smartphone-free zone, and other accessories to make this space attractive enough so other kids will want to purchase it. After explaining the concept, discuss:

- What is the largest challenge with this business?
- How many units would it be possible to sell in a month?
- If you were to start this venture, do you think it would be successful?

54 - Learn to do a SWOT analysis.

The classical SWOT analysis is one of the most basic analyses in business. You can teach this technique to your kid while making it fun and interesting.

You first need to find the right arena. It may be a local restaurant, a grocery store, a company in the neighborhood, the company where you work, or a media company. Start by talking in general terms about what the company does to earn money.

Then, take a sheet of paper and draw a cross in the middle, splitting the sheet into four squares. Each square on the paper represents one of the following words:

- S – STRENGTH – Write that word at the top of the upper-left square. Then start to discuss all the strengths of the business. Some strengths include what the company does well and the resources it has. Does the company have unique employees, a great location, fantastic marketing, a strong culture, new technology, and so on? As your kid comes up with points, you write them into the strength box.

- W – WEAKNESS – Write this word at the top of the upper-right square. After completing the strengths exercise, it's easier to continue with weaknesses. Try to come up with as many weak points as you did for the company's strengths. It's a good exercise for kids to consider what can be improved in a business model.

- O – OPPORTUNITIES – In the lower-left quadrant, write opportunities. In the square, write all the possible new directions the company should consider in the future. Here you have ample opportunities to be creative. Opportunities may include: selling more items to the same customers, selling to new customers, offering new products and services, expanding the company's reach into new markets, hiring more people, etc.

- T- THREATS – In the last quadrant, consider what can lead to the business declining or even going out of business. Write threats at the top of this square. Here you include new technology, new competitors, changes in society, etc.

You can also extend the SWOT analysis and make it personal. Maybe it's safest to start with you. What are the strengths, weaknesses, opportunities, and threats in your life?

You can do the same exercise with your kid's traits, but don't spend too much time on their weaknesses.

55 - The Not To-do list for kids.

Just as To-do lists are an essential tool for many adults in business and life, a Not To-do list may offer even more valuable lessons.

Over breakfast on the weekend, discuss this concept with your kid.

Then, ask your kid to make a Not To-do list for the day with activities and checkboxes beside each item. When you put activities on the list, you can have lots of good discussions. Challenge them on what they should not spend their time on during the day. Is your kid eliminating or limiting time spent on YouTube, social media, Netflix, etc.?

Have your kid keep the list with them throughout the day and check off avoided activities as the day progresses. There are apps to track how they spend their time when on their smartphone.

At night before going to bed, look at the list together to see how many activities were avoided. If activities are unchecked, you can discuss if the plan was too ambitious. On the other hand, should your kid have set the Not To-do goals higher if all the items on the list were avoided?

With all the extra time freed up during the day, discuss how your kid should fill the time with meaningful activities.

56 - Play the game Rise of Industry.

In the computer game Rise of Industry, you are a tycoon starting with a sum of money and the ambition to build an industrial empire.

As an entrepreneur, you build production means like factories, manage logistics to move raw materials, and produce finished goods to trade between cities.

The game has lots of strategic complexity to challenge and encourage you to learn how to think like an entrepreneur and business tycoon.

57 - Build a candy factory.

The book Charlie and the Chocolate Factory inspires kids all over the world to be creative. Now, you can use the lessons from this book as a fun exercise to teach your kid about business. Here is how to do it:

- *The idea* – Tell your kid to be creative and come up with ideas for new candy products. The goal should be to develop 4 to 8 new types of candy, chocolate, etc. If your kids like to draw, have him/her make a drawing of the sweets. The ideas do not have to be realistic. Let them use their creativity to come up with wild ideas.

- *Names* – Challenge your kid to come up with magical names for their new candy and a cool name for the factory. A unique name will help to make the products and business come alive.

- *Logo* – A company needs a logo. Have your kid draw their company's logo or create one on a computer. Use a presentation program like Microsoft PowerPoint or a dedicated drawing program like Adobe Illustrator or Canva. Experiment with different fonts, colors, and possibly a symbol to represent your business.

- *The cost* – What does it cost to produce your candy? Have the kid research online to find the production cost of similar sweets. Then have him/her estimate the unit cost of the candy.

- *The distribution model* – How will you sell the candy? From your own candy stores and website, or through other stores? Discuss the advantages and disadvantages of both approaches. The benefits of selling the sweets yourself are that you are in full control and keep all the profits from the sales. The advantage of selling through others is that those stores already have a distribution of sellers, making it's easier. Candy products have high margins. The retailer may expect to have a markup between 2.5 and 5, which means buying the candy for $1 and selling it between $2.50 and $5.

- *The price* – Discuss what the candy should cost for end customers. To get the price right, do research on what competitors charge for their candies. At the same time, consider the distribution model. If the difference between your cost and the price to end consumers is small, it's not possible to sell to other stores.

- *The TV advertisement* – Tell your kid that his/her factory has received $1 million to spend on TV advertisement. Have them draw how the advertisement will look and write a script for each scene. Tell them to illustrate the ad like a comic strip.

- *The investment* – Have your kid consider the cost of setting up the factory. How much does it cost to build? Then, consider the machines needed for candy production, packaging, etc. Help your kid guess at these expenses. When you have the total cost, discuss how to finance the venture. Is it possible to receive a loan from a bank? The answer is probably "no." Finding investors is another alternative. If a person invests $1 million in your venture, how much ownership do they receive?

Would you be willing to quit your job and your kid to leave school to pursue the candy factory full time?

58 - How to read a balance sheet.

A balance sheet is a financial statement showing all the company's assets on one side and their liabilities on the other. The two sides are always equal and balanced.

To illustrate this concept, use the example of your household. Take a sheet of paper and draw a line down the center. On the top of one column, write assets, and on the other side write liabilities. Your assets are everything you own and may include your house, car, clothes, furniture, etc. The liability column includes the debt accrued and the equity saved up from your salaries, etc., over the years.

Since your kid now has a vague understanding of the concept, you are ready to look at a real balance sheet together. Search for *company balance sheets* online. Have a look at a few items to get a greater understanding of how it works.

For assets:

- *Account receivables* – This includes the money the company will receive from customers and others who owe the company money.
- *Inventory* – If a company is selling products and has products in stock, the value of the stock inventory is found here. Consulting and legal companies, for example, sell services and have no assets under inventory.

- *Cash* – This includes the money a company currently has in its bank accounts.
- *Tangible assets* – Under tangible assets, you have the value of the company's property, machines, etc.
- *Intangible assets* – These are the assets you cannot see. It may include patents, and something called goodwill, which often comes from acquiring other companies.

Now on to the liabilities:

- *Current liabilities* - These are short-term commitments that you have promised to pay your suppliers, employees, etc.
- *Long-term liabilities* - Here, the value of long-term loans is recorded.
- *Shareholder equity* - Shareholder equity is what the owners have invested in the business over the years. It includes the initial sum invested in the company and all the earnings retained in the company.

59 - How to measure a business?

Just as there are grades in school, companies give grades to themselves to measure their performance and compare themselves to other similar companies. Ask your kid to come up with ways a company can measure its performance.

It's a fun and reflective exercise that you can have almost anywhere, like in the car or at the breakfast table. Here are some ideas to discuss:

- *Company value* – If the company is listed on a stock exchange, the company value is set by the market every day. It's an important measure that most companies try to maximize.

- *Revenues/Sales* – All companies measure their income in cash and in units (if they make physical products.) Revenues tell the company how popular their products or services are among its customers. Ask your kid if it's possible to manipulate the number. The answer is "yes." Companies move revenues from one time period to the next and can sometimes position business intentions as revenues.

- *Profit/EBITDA* – This measure tells if the company is profitable and is, for many, the ultimate measure of success.

- *Cash flow* – Even if a company is profitable, it may run out of cash to fund its operation. That's why companies are constantly measuring their cash flows.

- *Customer satisfaction and returns* – Companies can measure how satisfied their customers are by sending out questionnaires. They can also measure if customers return to buy more products or if they ask for refunds on their purchases.

- *The number of visitors/downloads/conversions* – If a company is running an online business, they will most likely track the number of visitors to their website, the number of downloaded documents/media files, etc., and finally, conversion. Conversion is the number of visitors that end up buying the product. A conversion rate of 2% means that 2 out of 100 visitors end up becoming customers.

- *Employee turnover* – Having happy employees is essential to most companies. It can be measured by questionnaires or by employee turnover. Turnover means how many employees quit during a year. If a company has 100 employees and 20 quit during a year, the turnover is 20%.

All of these measures have their advantages and disadvantages and can be manipulated. Most companies focus on 2 to 5 of these items per year to steer their company in a positive direction.

60 - What is the best idea - grass cutting or fruit/berry picking?

Ask your kid what business they would like to start. A lawn mowing business where they cut grass for neighbors or picking fruit and berries and selling it from a stand at their farmer's market.

If you go into lawn mowing, you will visit all the neighbors with a yard or garden and ask if you can cut their grass. You set a price per hour or a flat price for completing the job.

You can pick apples, strawberries, mushrooms, and wildflowers for free. The healthy, local food may be sold by knocking on doors or from a stand. Here are a few questions to probe the reasoning of your kid's decision:

- Which business is the most fun to start?
- Where would you make the most money?
- What is the easiest to start?
- Do these businesses have the same customers or are they different?

For the business, you like the best: How would you set up your business? What would be your prices? Which customers would you sell to? How would you do the marketing? Would you make a website?

What will it take for your kid to start this business the next weekend?

61 - How to serve a shit sandwich?

Your kid should be able to know a shit sandwich when they see one. It's one of the most classical approaches to giving feedback. The rationale for the feedback structure (sandwich) is to start with something nice to ease them into the conversation, then give the tough feedback before you end the conversation on a positive note.

Ask your kid if he/she knows what it is. When they answer is "no," ask if they want one, and then you serve them one.

Start by telling them how impressed you are with their schoolwork or something else they do well. Now that you put down the bottom bread slice, you're ready for the meat itself—the reason for the feedback. Say that you're disappointed with the mess in their room. It must change, and you expect him/her to take it seriously and improve (or anything else you want to criticize). Then, you place the sweet bread slice on top of the sandwich by telling them how much you care or that you appreciate a few of the other things they do around the house.

Discuss what just happened. Did he/she understand what a shit sandwich is from your example?

Having served the shit sandwich to your kid, turn the tables and let your kid then try to serve you one.

62 - How does a bank work?

Banks are central to the world economy. It makes sense to have a rudimentary understanding of how a bank operates.

Tell your kid that they now own a bank. What should they do to run the bank?

- First, who are the bank's customers? For most banks, the answer is easy. They have customers, private and businesses that give them money (depositors) and lenders.
- How does the bank make money and pay their employees? Banks pay less interest to the depositors than to the lenders, and they pay their expenses with the difference.
- How does a bank lose money? In most instances, banks unknowingly loan money to customers that cannot pay them back.
- What are the implications for entrepreneurship? The worst thing a bank can do is to loan large sums to customers who cannot pay them back later. Since most entrepreneurs fail, it does not make sense for banks to grant a loan unless the entrepreneur gives the bank an asset they can sell if the business fails. (Most often, the asset entrepreneurs have to use as a guarantee is real estate).

63 - Is selling spaghetti-filled pancakes at school a great idea?

Ask your kid if they think it's a good idea to start a venture that makes pancakes filled with spaghetti Bolognese and sell them at school?

The kid would prepare the treat at night, pack them the next morning, and sell them to school friends. After explaining the concept, discuss:

- What is the largest challenge with this business?
- How many filled pancakes would it be possible to sell in a month? How much money will you make?
- If you were to start this venture, do you think it would be successful?

64 - Your school has to buy a product from you. What do they buy?

Ask your kid what they would do if they had to develop a product or service for their school to buy.

What are some of the problems you have heard your teachers complain about? Can you do anything to help solve these problems?

What do you see as smart solutions for making life easier for teachers and students? What are some of your ideas to make the school more fun and safer for students?

65 - How many razor blades are sold?

There are many fun exercises to test your kid's reasoning and business judgment skills. Ask your kids, "How many razor blades are sold in our town, country, etc.?" The purpose of this exercise is not to calculate a correct answer but to train your kid's brain on the ability to structure a complex problem. Here's one way to tackle it:

- Start by considering how many people live in the area you selected. Let your kid guess, and then help him/her use reason to get to an approximate number.

- Then determine the age span of when people shave. Most people will say they shave from the age of 16 until they die. With a life expectancy of 78 years, it means you can reduce the number of people shaving by about 20%. Help your kid calculate the remaining population.

- Not all people use razors with blades. Some people use electric razors that do not have a traditional blade. The question is, how many people use these types of shavers? Help your kid estimate the number of people to remove from the razor blade population.

- Then, split the remaining population between men and women. Estimate how often men switch blades and multiply it by the number of men, and then women.

- Voila! You have calculated the number of razor blades sold in a year.

66 - Is a company that's losing money worth zero?

This can be the starting point of an interesting discussion.

Losing or making money has little to do with the overall value of a company.

All else equal, a company making money is worth more than a company losing money, but the value has much more to do with the company's prospects rather than the current results.

Tesla and Amazon are examples of companies that lost money for a long time while still having a high valuation.

On stock listing sites, you can look up the profit of different companies. Examine the valuation of companies losing money. Why are they so high or low?

67 - Why offer a money-back guarantee?

Many companies offer money-back guarantees.

Visit a few different company's websites to study their guarantees. What do they say to customers and why?

Discuss with your kid why companies offer these types of guarantees, and what they believe the cost is to the company. Here are some points to keep in mind:

- Most companies offer these guarantees to reduce consumers' anxiety and to convert visitors into buying customers.

- Guarantees signal quality and a company's belief in their products and services. Guarantees encourage customers to think, "The company would not offer these guarantees if they were not confident in their products and services."

- How much money does the guarantee cost the company? To calculate it, discuss how many customers actually use the guarantee to get their money back. If you assume that 2% of customers seek their money back, and you have to throw away 50% of the products they return, then the cost to the company is 1% of the product cost.

68 - How to solve your friend's problems?

Problems are great opportunities to start new ventures. A problem means that there's possibly a customer willing to pay money for your solution. The solution may either be a product or a service. Tell your kid to focus on their friend's problems and the challenges they face. This is a useful exercise in empathy, out-of-the-box thinking, and how to develop ideas, or brainstorm. Here's how to set it up:

- Write "large problems," "small problems," "frequent problems," and "infrequent problems," in four columns on a sheet of paper.
- Then, start asking probing questions to help your kid identify problems. What does their friend's day look like? What are their struggles? What help do they need?

When you have written ten problems on the paper, go into problem-solving mode to tackle the following questions:

- Is the solution to the problem a product or a service?
- Is the solution something kids can create and deliver?
- Will your friends pay for the solution?

Write the answer to each of these questions on the paper next to each problem. Next time your kid spends time with their friend, have them bring the results from this exercise along and discuss the problems and solutions.

69 - What is upselling?

Ask your kids if they can remember if they have been up-sold?

You will probably get a blank stare.

Upselling means that instead of purchasing the product that you intended, the seller is trying to convince you to buy something more expensive.

In many stores, employees are encouraged to look for opportunities to upsell. They might say to you, "The TV you want is good but have a look at this one! It has all these new features, and it's an outstanding value."

The rationale for upselling is to increase sales or have customers purchase a product with better margins for the retailer.

After explaining this business practice to your kid, count how many times a month you experience upselling—and how many times you fall for it!

70 - Watch The Pursuit of Happiness together.

This wonderfully touching movie has many lessons for business and life. Watch the movie with your kid and have a discussion afterward. Here are some of the lessons to talk about:

- *Have the courage to set high aspirations* – Having high aspirations may motivate and guide your pursuits. In the movie, Will Smith's character aspires to become a stockbroker while he is living in hardship on the streets.
- *Never give up* – Your circumstances may be challenging, but never give up. Will Smith's character faces one tough situation after another but maintains a positive attitude and works hard towards his goal.
- *Don't let other people's opinions stop you* – In the movie, the people around Will Smith's character believe his ambition is too optimistic and not realistic, but he doesn't listen and presses on.
- *Work hard and show up* – The movie shows the importance of working hard and showing up, even though you may be experiencing hardship in your life.

71 - Play Monopoly together.

Monopoly is a board game that brings out the best and worst of kids and adults alike. Give it a try, but instead of only focusing on winning, discuss what business you can learn from the game:

- The most expensive property is not necessarily the best because they are costly to buy and expensive to maintain. Although adding a hotel at one of these properties in your game play can deliver a knockout punch, they might ruin your cash flow and hinder you from purchasing other properties.

- Be patient. Beginner players often buy all the property they land on and run out of money. Pro players have more of a strategy and only buy specific properties and play the long and patient game.

- Focus on your money and cash flow. Monopoly is an easy game. You start out with some money, and when the game ends, whoever has the most money left is the winner. Keeping an eye on cash flow, properties, and future potential is the key. The best value on the board is to buy the railroads. If you own all four stations, you receive a high interest on the money you spent to acquire them.

- Diversification is a concept from the business world that means that you should not put all your eggs into one basket (or all of your money into one thing). The same rule applies to Monopoly. Usually, the winner is someone who spreads out their investments on the board and does not count on one property alone to earn them revenue.
- Keep cash available. If you are investing too heavily in assets, you might soon end up penniless.
- You need to take some risk. If you just keep the cash without investing, you will soon have to pay up to other people who own the properties you come across on the game board. Remember, at the end of the game, staying in jail can be smart because moving around the board is expensive.

72 - Watch Moneyball together.

Moneyball is a fun movie with an ensemble of talented actors, including Brad Pitt. The movie has valuable lessons for business and life:

- *Think differently* – When you don't have a large budget, you need to think differently. The baseball team in the movie has certain limitations that force them to rethink how to create a winning team.

- *The importance of numbers* – Focus on data. It doesn't lie. In the movie, the team not only focuses on readily available data but also invests in different types of data that give them new insights to make better decisions.

- *Believe in yourself and the system* – People might doubt you, and success does not come overnight, so you have to believe in yourself.

73 - What is the best idea - become a magician or balloon maker?

Ask your kid what business they would like to start. Becoming a magician performing at birthdays or acting as a balloon maker creating crazy cool balloons on birthdays.

Being a magician is fun but demanding. You have to learn a great routine to perform at birthday parties in your area. You charge the parents for each of your performances. If the venture is successful, you can even perform at adult parties.

Making balloon animals and other figures is great fun and something young kids love. It doesn't take that long to master, and you can sell your service to parents in the neighborhood.

Here are a few questions to probe their reasoning:

- Which business do you think will be the most fun to start? Where would you make the most money? What is the easiest to start? Do these businesses have the same customers or are they different?

- For the business, you like the best: How would you set up your business? What would be your prices? Which customers would you sell to? How would you do the marketing? Would you make a website? What will it take for your kid to start this business the next weekend?

74 - Is personalized books for kids a good idea?

Ask your kid if they think it's a good idea to start a venture creating personalized books for young kids where the hero of the story has the same name as the kid and all the action takes place in their familiar neighborhood. You can sell it as an electronic book or have it printed. After explaining the concept, discuss:

- What is the largest challenge with this business?
- How many books would it be possible to sell in a month?
- If you were to start this venture, do you think it would be successful?

75 - How much does TV advertisement cost?

TV advertising is exciting, and many people wonder if it's expensive.

The answer is "yes" and "no."

The cost of running an ad depends on a few factors. The most important factor is how many viewers are watching your ad. Running ads during the Super Bowl or during the Olympics are famous for being expensive because of its prestige and millions of viewers. The cost can be above $5 million per commercial spot.

On the other hand, running a TV ad on a smaller channel or during the middle of the night can cost only a few hundred dollars.

Then, there's the cost of producing the TV ad. A few years ago, the production costs for TV ads cost millions of dollars, but it's now possible to produce ads at a much lower cost.

76 - How does a YouTuber make money?

Your kid probably watches a lot of YouTube. Ask them if they know how the YouTuber makes money from posting videos online. This is an excellent exercise to make your kid aware of how they are influenced by people and companies:

- *Advertisements* – YouTube makes money on the ads shown before, during, and after the content. Some content creators have an agreement with YouTube where they earn a few dollars per 1,000 views. For this reason, YouTubers want views and subscribers, and their subscribers are notified when a new video is available.

- *Product placement* – A YouTuber can talk about a product or company in demonstrations, unboxings, or products may be subtly placed in the background of their video. The YouTuber gets paid by the company when they show the product on their videos and or sending their viewers to the company's website with a discount code to buy the product.

- *Partnerships and sponsors* – The YouTuber's episode can have a sponsor or companies can sponsor the YouTuber. The more subscribers, the more money they can earn from paid partnerships.

Watch a few YouTube videos with your kid and see if you can spot all the ways the YouTuber is making money through their video content.

77 - What is the market for house cleaning services?

This is a fun reasoning exercise. Ask your kid, "what is the market for house cleaning for families at your school?"

- Start by guessing the number of students in school.
- Since you want to approximate the number of households, remove students who live together like brothers and sisters. Maybe it adds up to 5%.
- Then, add the number of parents who do not live in the same house (like those who are divorced). This means that one kid is part of two households. Maybe it adds up to 10%.
- How many of these households don't clean their own house? Make assumptions. It's the reasoning for this number that matters, not that it is an exact figure.
- For households hiring cleaning services, how frequently are they cleaning? Approximate the answer and calculate the number of cleans per year.
- Finally, on average what do they spend per cleaning?
- Now you have all you need. Take "the average sum per cleaning," multiply it by "cleanings per year," then multiply it by "the number of households that use professional cleaning services." Now you have the total market for house cleaning.

78 - What is the purpose of a business?

Understanding the purpose of business is an excellent starting point for a discussion with your kid.

- Decades ago, the business of business was to create shareholder value. In this paradigm, as an investor, you don't want the company to spend money on charity or other positive measures. The company pays taxes and returns the money to shareholders. Then, it was up to the investors to spend the earned money on whatever they wanted, including good causes.

- Over time, the purpose of business has become more nuanced. Today, some companies have charitable causes incorporated into their product like Toms Shoes, which gives away one pair of shoes for every pair they sell. Other companies have decided to pay suppliers more money if they are more environmentally friendly or uphold more ethical practices than other suppliers.

- If your kid likes contributing to good causes, discuss how much a company should gives away. Do they think that investors are interested in being a part of a company that donates so much time and money? If stakeholders no longer like the investment, the company's value drops, which may lead to severe troubles for the company in the future.

79 - How will companies fare if a catastrophe occurs in the world?

This is a serious yet interesting exercise to do. From time to time, catastrophes happen. When they do, they have a huge negative impact on some companies and a positive impact on others. Some effects are easy to understand (called primary effects), while secondary effects are much harder to predict. Consider these catastrophe scenarios with your kid:

- *A health pandemic hits the world* – Which companies will be most severely affected, and why? This is an interesting exercise after experiencing the Covid-19 pandemic as a family. Try to ask your kid some unexpected questions. What happens to computer game companies, toy companies, ice cream companies, etc., when a pandemic hits?

- *Terrorists fly airplanes into the World Trade Center in New York City* – Which companies will be hit hardest by this attack, and why? Some companies will do well. For instance, who might benefit from people traveling less? Trying to reason around these effects can teach you how society and business are interconnected.

- *The housing market falls 30%* – Which companies will be hit hardest, and why? In many countries, the wealth of the households is linked to housing prices. If families suffer financially, will they spend less on food, trips to Disneyland, or clothes? Why?

80 - What is the best idea - dog walking or plant watering business?

Ask your kid what business they would like to start between a dog walking business or a plant watering business.

In a dog walking business, your kid would take dogs in the neighborhood for a walk a few times per week and on the weekends. They could choose to walk one dog at a time or multiple dogs simultaneously.

A plant watering business means that your kid waters the plants of families on vacation. The kid goes to their neighbor's house a few times and makes sure all the plants survive while the owners travel.

Questions to probe the reasoning of your kid's decision:

- Which business will be the most fun to start?
- Where would you make the most money?
- What is the easiest to start?
- Do these businesses have the same customers or are they different?
- For the business, you like the best: How would you set up your business? What would be your prices? Which customers would you sell to? How would you do the marketing? Would you make a website?

What will it take for your kid to start this business the next weekend?

81 - How to value a company?

There are many misconceptions when it comes to the value of a company. Some people believe the higher the stock price, the higher the company's value. This is not true. Ask your kid, "How would you value a company?" The question may have many answers. Here are some ideas to discuss:

- For publicly traded companies (those listed on a stock exchange,) the value of the company is whatever the buyers and sellers agree on. People who sell a stock sell because they believe the stock's value will go down, whereas the buyers think its value will go up. They meet at the stock price, and when multiplying it by the number of shares, you get the value of the company.

- You can compare a stock to owning a house. The house has value, and you can rent it out for a cash flow. The same is true for companies. Companies have assets that may include machines, products, brands, people, etc. These assets can be valuable, but the real value is how much profit those assets make for the company. A common way for investors to value a company is to say it's worth 5 to 20 times the yearly profit, depending on the type of company, market, growth, etc. The way to frame it is to say, how much do you think it's worth to get $1,000 a year for the next 20 years. The answer is not $20,000 since it's better to have $20,000 today than to have it spread out over many years.

82 - Watch Big starring Tom Hanks together.

You have probably seen the classic film *Big* starring Tom Hanks. It's a great movie to watch with your kid, and it holds many lessons for life and business. Here are some of the lessons to discuss after watching the movie.

- *Don't let other people's opinions influence your own* – Always speak your mind. When the kid is asked for his opinion in the movie, he always answers in a frank and straightforward manner. The feedback becomes very valuable to the company.

- *Question, question, and question* – During many discussions with the company's executives, the kid keeps asking "why" until he gets to the truth or the underlying assumptions of the conversation. Keeping asking and you will soon get some valuable answers.

- *Be yourself* – As the movie progresses, the kid starts behaving more like an adult and loses the qualities that make him unique and authentic. He finally understands what makes him unique and gets back to his usual self.

83 - Is buying used Legos and reselling them a great idea?

Ask your kid if they think it's a good idea to start a venture buying old Legos that are just lying around in other kids' drawers and under their beds. You can weigh the Lego and pay them a fixed sum per kilo or pound.

Once the Legos are purchased, you can bring them home to clean and create a system for organizing the Lego pieces before selling them to other kids in the neighborhood or online.

After explaining the concept, discuss:

- What is the biggest challenge with this business?
- How many Legos would it be possible to sell in a month?
- How much money will you make?
- If you were to start this venture, do you think it would be successful?

84 - Is developing and selling the ultimate super soaker a great idea?

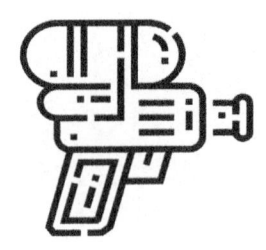

Ask your kid if they think it's a good idea to start a venture building and selling the ultimate super soaker by adapting a large, standardized water gun.

The soaker is so powerful that it can hurt people if they stand too close when it's fired. You sell the soaker to customers at school or in your community.

After explaining the concept, discuss:

- What is the largest challenge with this business?
- How many super soakers would it be possible to sell in a month? How much money might you make?
- If you were to start this venture, do you think it would be successful?

85 - What is the best business idea - car washer or bicycle fixer?

Ask your kid what business they would like to start between becoming a car washer providing clean cars to the entire neighborhood or being the bicycle fixer that maintains all bikes and makes them shine. Cars need regular washing to maintain their exterior. It's a problem that most adults face. Their problem is your opportunity. Besides cleaning the outside of the car, you can consider cleaning the inside of the vehicles by vacuuming the rugs, dusting the consoles, and cleaning the windows. Bikes need maintenance, and many adults don't know how to do it. If you are hand at fixing bikes and putting air in the tires it can be great fun, and a service you can charge money for. Here are a few questions to probe their reasoning:

- Which business will be the most fun to start?
- Where would you make the most money?
- What is the easiest to start?
- Do these businesses have the same customers?
- For the business, you like the best: How would you set up your business? What would be your prices? Which customers would you sell to? How would you do the marketing? Would you make a website?

What will it take for your kid to start this business the next weekend?

86 - Is a gift advice business a great idea?

Ask your kid if they think it's a good idea to start a venture advising parents on what gifts to buy for their kids.

With your kid's expertise in what children want and where to buy it, they are often the perfect solution to parents' problems. They can charge the parents 5 dollars per piece of advice. After explaining the concept, discuss:

- What is the largest challenge with this business?
- How many parents would it be possible to sell their services to in a month?
- How much money might you make?
- If you were to start this venture, do you think it would be successful?

87- Arrange a business playdate for your kid and their friends.

When your kid has a friend over at your house, they often complain that they have nothing to do. Now you have an answer. It's the perfect opportunity for them to create a fun business together. Here are some ideas to get their creativity flowing:

- *Holding a yard sale* – Let the kids take toys and household items no longer in use and put them on a table outside your home. They then try to sell the items for a fair price to people passing by. Make sure you approve all of the items they intend to sell.

- *Setting up a waffle and lemonade stand* – Have the kids make a batch of waffles and a pitcher of lemonade and set up a stand in front of your house. Will they be able to sell some of their products to people walking by? Make sure the foods are made safely and hygienically.

- *Selling fruit and berries* – Let the kids pick fruit and berries in local groves that they can sell to neighbors or at local farmer's markets.

- *Creating cool marketing posters* – Decide on a business idea with the kids. Then, have them create a fantastic marketing poster explaining their business and offers.

- *Creating a sales brochure* – Decide on a business idea with the kids. Then, have them fold an A4 piece of paper to create a four-page sales brochure. They fill the pages with all of the information they believe is necessary to convince customers to buy their offerings. The content may be headlines, drawings, sales pitches, prices, pictures, and so on.

- *The name and logo challenge* – Decide on a business idea together and have the kids come up with a name for the venture. Then, they create logos for the company on their computer or by drawing on paper.

- *The YouTube channel plan* – Tell the kids to plan a YouTube channel they can launch together. What will the channel focus upon? Will there be guests, and who are their dream candidates? Can they think of companies that may sponsor them? What type of viewers would they want to watch their videos (other kids, moms, etc.)? Finally, have them prepare a pilot episode you can watch together.

- *The investor pitch* – Have the kids come up with an idea for a new venture. Then, they create a business plan and prepare a pitch to an investor. When they are ready to present, let them pitch to you and tell them why or why not you would consider inventing funds into this company based on their presentation.

88 - What is the best business idea - helping seniors or cleaning houses?

Ask your kid what business they would like to start between a service for seniors where they help senior citizens with their daily needs or a house cleaning venture where they clean houses in the neighborhood. Seniors usually need more help than other people with chores around the house, grocery shopping, etc. You can provide that service and make good money while having a positive impact on your neighbors' lives.

Everyone needs to clean their house, often many times a month, and lucky for you, people hate cleaning. That's your opportunity to start a house cleaning service for customers in your neighborhood. Here are a few questions to probe the reasoning of your kid's decision:

- Which business will be the most fun to start?
- Where would you make the most money?
- What is the easiest to start?
- Do these businesses have the same customers?
- For the business, you like the best: How would you set up your business? What would be your prices? Which customers would you sell to? How would you do the marketing? Would you make a website?

What will it take for your kid to start this business the next weekend?

89 - How to structure a retail store?

Walking around in local stores are great starting places for fun and interesting business discussions with your kid.

Why has the company created this layout for their store? The layout means where different categories of products are located in the store's blueprint. It's not random, as a store's design is a science where little is left to chance. Use supermarkets as examples:

- Pose the question to your kid, "why are flowers and fruit close to the entrance?" They are pretty, smell and look good and signals that other products in the store are fresh and of good quality.
- Why are the baked goods often right behind the fruits and flowers? Breads and cakes make you hungry. Science shows that a hungry shopper spends more money on their groceries.
- Why are dairy products placed in the back of the store? These are items customers need and buy often. By placing them in the back of the store, the supermarket hopes that customers might pick up several impulse-buys on their way to get milk.
- Why are candy and magazines placed close to the registers? If stores have impulse products like these close to the exit, they can turn customers' "waiting time into buying time."

- Is it best to place your product on the shelves or on the endcaps of the aisles? Endcaps are the best, and suppliers often have to pay extra to have their products placed at the endcaps.
- Where do you want your product to be positioned on a shelf?
    - *Eye-level* – The saying "eye-level is buy-level" holds true. In many stores, the suppliers are paying good money to be positioned in the middle of the shelf.
    - *Top-level* – Here, you will most often find smaller and more unknown brands. They end up on the top shelves due to their smaller sales and because the supplier often can't afford to buy the better shelf placement.
    - *Bottom-level* – This zone is often used to display new brands and for products that take up a lot of shelf space (like toilet paper, etc.).
- *Cross merchandising* – This tactic means that the store co-locates products that belong together in the consumer's mind but are actually from different retail categories. Examples may be ketchup shelved next to hotdogs and batteries shelved next to toys, etc.

To get your kid thinking, ask what advice they would give to the store managers about arranging the products in the store.

90 - The five whys of business.

Other people's problems are a source of new ideas. A way to dig deep into problems and solutions is the five whys method.

The method is straightforward: Ask "why" five times in a row. By doing this exercise, you will soon reach the core sources of the problems, new opportunities, and possible solutions.

It's a great exercise to perform with potential customers of the venture or your kid on other issues. Here is an example of the five whys method:

- "I want to start my own venture."
- "Why?"
- "Because it will give me flexibility."
- "Why is flexibility important?"
- "Because then I can work from home."
- "Why is it important to work from home?"
- "Because then I can take care of my dad."
- "Why do you want to take care of your dad?"
- "Because he is very important to me."
- "Why is he important to you?"
- "Because he taught me about entrepreneurship."

91 - Create a subscription business.

Many entrepreneurs like subscription businesses because they provide a more stable income and allow you to sell more to existing customers rather than chase new ones. Also, these businesses can be very profitable. Examples of subscription businesses are: movie and music streaming, online courses, smartphone data plans, etc.

Challenge your kid to come up with an idea for a new venture based on the subscription model. A few starter questions are:

- What ideas do they have for subscriptions? Spend time discussing the differences between selling a product or service one time versus selling that service repeatedly as a subscription. Examples of a repeat offering might be selling fresh, warm rolls on Sundays, a lawn mowing service where customers pay per month to have their grass cut, and a computer help service where you make sure that your customers' technological gadgets work properly for a fixed fee per month.
- How much money would they charge for product or service subscription?
- How many customers will they have, a couple of months into the venture? Does your kid like the idea of starting a subscription business, and if so, will he/she start one?

92 - How to make the investor pitch?

Most startup companies that need to raise money from investors have to do an investor pitch.

Now it's your kid's turn. This exercise will teach your kid how to communicate with other people and prepare and present their main point. Here's how to set up this exercise:

- Together with your kid, decide on a business idea and plan that he/she can pitch.
- Decide who will be present at the pitch. Will it just be you or will other family members and friends attend?
- Develop the investor pitch. Here's what a pitch should include:
  - The description of the business concept.
  - The target customer.
  - The size of the market.
  - The sales numbers (how much they expect to sell) and the profits from it.
  - The investment size they want from you, and how much of the company they will give up for that investment.

After the pitch, you can ask more questions, but remember, building your kid's confidence and presentation ability is the most important point of the exercise.

93 - How to evaluate ideas?

There are billions of ideas out there. Most are bad, as can be seen by the number of new businesses and initiatives that fail.

At the same time, some of the world's best ideas seemed bad for a long amount of time before they suddenly became great by all business and social standards.

J.K. Rowling's first Harry Potter manuscript was turned down 12 times before a publisher bought it. Jeff Bezos of Amazon attended 68 meetings to raise his first million dollars because very few investors thought that selling books online was a good idea.

Airbnb and Uber were considered crazy ideas for a long time until they took off. And just look at the YouTubers making millions of dollars each day! Would you have guessed that their channel would become a massive success?

Since it's so difficult to judge if an idea has potential or not, the criteria for evaluating ideas must be taken with a grain of salt. When discussing ideas with your kid, consider asking these questions to test the quality of the ideas:

- Does the product or service fix a problem that many people have? The more people who have the problem, the better.

- Solving a tough problem is better than solving small problems. This leads to a dilemma when seen in conjunction with the previous point: Is it better to solve a tough problem few people have or a small problem many have? There is no right answer to this query. But some investors prefer ventures that attempt to solve tough problems that few people have in one market and then expand the venture into new geographical markets to gain more customers.
- Are there many competing solutions to the problem, and if so, how is your idea better or different from others?
- Are the customers willing to pay to have their problem solved, and if so, are they willing to spend enough money to make your venture profitable?
- Is it a good idea for you to pursue? Do you have what it takes to make the vision come alive? A smaller smartphone with a better battery may be a good idea, but not for you if you do not have the skill set to solve that problem.

94 - Should you create an app for household duties?

Most parents and kids fight about doing the household chores. What if your kid developed a smartphone app that makes doing housework fun, interesting, and rewarding?

Discuss how to build the app with your kids. Even though you may decide not to build it, the exercise will give you both some valuable lessons. Here are the steps:

- *The problem* – What problem or problems are you trying to solve? It can be many, and if you are not clear, the solutions may go in all directions. Is the problem that kids don't know how to perform housework? Is it that the kids forget to do their tasks, so parents have to constantly remind them to do their chores? Are the kids unmotivated, or is there no accountability and reward for completing their chores?

- *The solution* – Match the most critical problem with a possible solution. If you decide that the problem is "parents are tired of nagging their kids to do housework, and kids want recognition and rewards for doing their part," then create an app that aims to provide the solution. In the app, parents may delegate tasks to family members with automatic reminders. When the kid has completed the task, he/she earns points in the app that are collected and can be saved up for future rewards.

- *The app* – If you decide to develop an app, you face many decisions. The first is to decide on the most important functionality of the app. Then, draw up the different steps of the user experience and mock-up screenshots of what the app's appearance and features are. There are free online programs to help you in this process. When completed, you'll have a rough design of the app.

- *The business model* – If you are launching an app, you have three business models to choose from to make money. You may sell the app to customers for a one-time fee, a recurring monthly fee, or allow the customer to download the app for free and advertisers pay for in-app ads. Today, many apps have both a free subscription with limited functionality to attract customers as well as a paid subscription option with more functionality.

- *Developing the app* – If you have a good and detailed design, it's easier to code and build the app. Building apps has become easier, but it makes sense to seek professional help if the project is ambitious. There are many app developers, and it should not be too difficult for them to estimate the cost of development.

- *Launching the app* – Some people believe that the most challenging part is to build the app, where other people think it's more difficult to make the app a success. Making the app popular is not an easy task. You need to collect positive reviews on the app stores and make them known through paid advertisement, public relations, and word of mouth.

Building an app is a super-challenging project that will teach you and your kid a lot about business, apps, and yourself. Be aware of the investment required to make it happen.

95 - Create a marketing campaign for school.

Imagine your kid's school decided they want to enroll more students and have asked you and your kid to help develop their marketing campaign. They give you $10,000 to make the campaign successful.

Now it's up to you and your kid to help the school achieve its goal. Together, you need to develop a marketing campaign and plan. You can discuss it with your kid, or even better, write it down. Here's how to do it:

- *The objective* – To prepare a marketing campaign, you need to first define the objective you want to achieve. In this instance, it's enrolling more students. You should strive to be even more concrete with the objective by defining precisely how many new students. Perhaps 100 new students could be a goal for this exercise.

- *The target customer* – Define who your marketing campaign targets. Is it the parents or students themselves? Will your message and selected media channel change depending upon whether you are communicating to the parents or the students? Why or why not? Make assumptions on your audience's preferred method of consuming information, and move on to the next step.

- *Communication* – What is the main theme of your campaign? This is the central idea of what you plan to say in your communications and messaging.
- *Marketing channels* – Which channels do you plan to use to reach the customers you defined as your "target customer." Marketing channels may include newspapers, magazines, direct mail (ads you get in your mailbox), radio, TV, social media, search engines, etc.
- *The ads* – After selected your communication channels, you need to design the advertising. Ads may include the message, the images, and the call to action (what you want the viewer to do after seeing the ad).

Now you have the marketing plan to present to your school.

Does it make sense, and will it achieve the school's goal?

96 - Is a parenting guide a good idea?

Ask your kid if they think it's a good idea to start a venture advising parents on the best ways to interact with their kids.

Most parents struggle with some aspect of raising or communicating with their kids.

Since your kid is a kid, he/she may provide a unique point of view and can give good advice to adults from a kid's perspective.

The venture may include selling a small booklet and then giving advice. The parents may pay by the hour for your kid's advice. After explaining the concept to your kid, discuss:

- What is the largest challenge with this business?
- How many advice sessions would it be possible to sell in a month?
- If you were to start this venture, do you think it would be successful?

97 - A/B testing with your kids.

A/B testing is an interesting business concept that has gained a lot of interest over the past ten years.

The idea is simple—test one element of a business against another in a controlled manner. By just changing one aspect at a time and measuring the effect, it's easier to see what works and what doesn't. Large companies like Google, Facebook, and Amazon run hundreds of these A/B tests, or split tests, each month.

Start an A/B test with a hypothesis. A hypothesis is an idea to improve the company. Then, set up the test and decide how to measure the effects. You then run the test, carefully measuring the different outcomes. The winner of the test becomes the new normal. Here's how to teach your kid about A/B testing:

- *Develop hypotheses* – Hypotheses are ideas for improvements. If you look at a headline in an ad, how can you improve it? Create a second ad with a new headline that you believe is better than the first headline and keep the rest of the ad identical to the first. You then show the two ads to different groups of people while measuring the ad's effects (like increased sales, decreased web traffic, etc.). Hypotheses come in all forms and shapes. Examples may be changing the font color of posters, the size of clickable buttons on a webpage, the price of one dish on a menu, etc.

- *Set up the experiments* – To test the hypothesis, you need to prepare an experiment. You can experiment in a parallel or sequential model. A lot of software lets you A/B test in parallel on webpages, meaning you show different versions of the ad to different customers at random and in parallel. On the other hand, if you have a lemonade stand and want to test what happens if you change the price from $2 to $3, you would do the test in sequence: one day displaying the $2 price and then the $3 price the next day. You then have to count the people passing by and the number of sales each day. Be aware that the larger the number of potential customers you show something to, the more confident you can be of the conclusion of your A/B test.

- *Change or stay the same* – Did your hypothesis lead to a better result, and then a change in how you operate? If not, then stay with what you have. Remember, there are valuable lessons to be learned in testing hypotheses that turn out to be wrong.

After introducing your kid to this concept, you can now apply it. Talk about your hypotheses for improvements when you read a magazine, walk into a store, or eat in a restaurant. Then, discuss how to test them.

98 - Become a master negotiator.

In business, as in life, being able to negotiate is an important skill. If you start a venture, you will need to know how to negotiate with customers, suppliers, and employees. Here are some fun exercises that will teach your kid valuable negotiation lessons for business and in life:

- Pretend that you are the customer, and your kid is selling strawberries at the farmer's market. It's 5 minutes before closing time. The strawberries are priced at $10 per basket, and he/she has 24 baskets left. You try to negotiate the best buying price, and your kid tries to get the best sales price. Negotiate until you get to a price where you both agree. Some techniques might include reminding them that the strawberries can't be sold tomorrow, that you are willing to buy all of the baskets if the price is right, etc.

- In this exercise, imagine your kid is a toy store owner, and you are an important supplier selling them 4 Lego sets priced at $10, $20, $30, and $40. Your kid tries to get the lowest price while you try to sell the sets at a high price. Negotiate until you come to an agreement.

- Imagine that your kid wants to buy 1,000 Pokémon cards from a person online. The person has offered the cards for $500, but in the messages going back and forth, you sense it's possible to negotiate the price down. How would you structure the negotiation?

- Your kid wants to cut grass for the summer to earn money. A neighbor intends to pay $10, but your kid wants $15. How should he/she negotiate with the neighbor?
- Your kid and five of his/her friends arrive at a local bakery just a few minutes before closing time. The chocolate croissants look really tasty. The bakery has 10 croissants left, at a normal price of $3 each. How should your kid negotiate to get the best price for all 10 croissants?

99- What is the best business idea - a tech wiz or website developer?

Ask your kid what business they would like to start. A tech wiz helping seniors and others in the neighborhood with their computers, stereos, smartphones, etc., or becoming a website developer assisting companies in setting up and maintaining their websites. Families need help using their technology. Your services can range from setting up equipment, to trouble-shooting problems, to holding training sessions. This is the perfect start-up for a tech wiz like you. Companies need help setting up and managing their websites and social media accounts. You will build and maintain their websites, and they will pay you by the hour or a fixed amount per month.

Here are questions to probe the reasoning of the decision:
- Which business will be the most fun to start?
- Where would you make the most money?
- What is the easiest to start?
- Do these businesses have the same customers?
- For the business, you like the best: How would you set up your business? What would be your prices? Which customers would you sell to? How would you do the marketing? Would you make a website?

What will it take for your kid to start this business the next weekend?

Please check out the other titles from Upstart Garage Media:

15 Great Ventures to Start (I)

15 Great Ventures to Start (II)

The YouTuber

The Waffle Maker

All rights reserved. This book or any portion thereof
may not be reproduced or used in any manner whatsoever
without the express written permission of the publisher
except for the use of brief quotations in a book review.

www.upstartgarage.com

Printed in Great Britain
by Amazon